HockeyNomics

What the Stats Really Reveal

Darcy Norman

OVER
TIME
BOOKS

The Publisher: OverTime Books is an imprint of Éditions de la Montagne Verte

Website: www.overtimebooks.com

Library and Archives Canada Cataloguing in Publication

Norman, Darcy, 1980–
        HockeyNomics: What the Stats Really Reveal / Darcy Norman.

Includes bibliographical references.
        ISBN: 978-1-897277-45-4

1. National Hockey League Statistics. 2. Hockey Statistics.
I. Title.

GV847.8.N3N67 2009   796.962'64021   C2009-903554-5

Project Director: J. Alexander Poulton
Project Editor: Carla MacKay
Cover Design: Joy Dirto
Cover Image: Courtesy of Dreamstime.com © Woodooart | Dreamstime.com (Ice Hockey Puck)

We acknowledge the financial support of the Government of Canada through the Book Publishing Industry Development Program for our publishing activities.

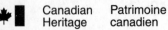

Canadian Heritage   Patrimoine canadien

PC: 1

Contents

Dedication

To my hockey friends, and our hours and
hours of argument.

Introduction

What is Hockeynomics? Clearly, it's a portmanteau of two words, so the most logical way to deal with it is to look at each word in turn.

The first one is easy. Hockey is Canada's national pastime, a fantastic, exciting game consisting of skates, sticks and a vulcanized piece of rubber. Depending on who you talk to, the word *hockey* can conjure up contrasting meanings: to a tyke-age player, it's how to get to the net without falling; to a midget-age player, it's how to pull the fanciest stickhandling moves; to an NHL player, it's how to get the Stanley Cup back to his hometown. The ideas are different, but the end objectives are always the same: scoring goals and winning games. From the time you lace up your first pair of skates, this main concept is made clear—skate down the ice, guide the puck with your stick, shoot when you get to the opponent's net.

Sure, there are obstacles along the way, and maybe even a penalty or two, but the basics don't change.

The second word is a bit tougher. Obviously, *nomics* comes from the word *economics*. Many people instinctively associate economics with money, but that's only partly correct. The textbook definition of economics is the science of dealing with the allocation of scarce resources. Because money is almost always one such resource, it's commonly part of any equation describing an economic problem. So economics can deal with money, but also with, well, anything.

What exactly do I mean by "allocating scarce resources"? Say you're a carrot farmer who only eats apples and walnuts. Each harvest, when you travel to the market, you sell carrots and buy apples and walnuts. Ideally, you would sell unlimited carrots and buy unlimited apples and walnuts every year. But that's impossible. There aren't enough vegetables, fruit and nuts to go around, therefore that kind of demand can't be met, and carrots, apples and walnuts are said to be "scarce resources." Instead, you have to find a balance between how many carrots you have to sell and how many apples and walnuts you need to buy. This allocation of food sales and purchases is an economic problem. Did you have a good harvest, hence many carrots?

Do you like apples more than walnuts, and if so, how much more? How much do *other* people value carrots, apples and walnuts? Somewhere in there is a particular solution to your problem, and economics hopes to deliver the answer.

Of course, this is a simplified definition, but economics provides statistical tools and theories that allow us to answer interesting questions, as well as arrive at the most efficient outcomes to problems. So when we combine the words *hockey* and *economics*, this is exactly what we get: the use of statistical tools and theories to answer interesting questions pertaining to the wonderful world of hockey. Is Martin Brodeur the best goaltender ever? Is there an easy way to compare players? Do the NHL award-winners deserve their trophies?

Hockeynomics, the field, can provide the answers.

Don't be intimidated. If you're a sports fan, you've been inundated by statistics and numbers your whole life. In this book, I hope to provide an introduction into the fascinating but relatively unknown realm of the statistical analysis of hockey. What is the state of the field, and how did we get to this point? Who's writing about this stuff? And most importantly: why should the average hockey fan care?

HockeyNomics, the book, can provide the answers.

Chapter One

Sports Statistics and Analysis: A History

Statistics and Sports

Statistics and sports are inseparable. It's nearly impossible to have a conversation about a hockey player or team without a statistic entering the fray. Quantifying an athlete's accomplishments makes description and comparison easier than purely qualitative means. Say someone asked you if Brett Hull was a good hockey player. How would you answer? You could describe all the qualities that made him a great player: his ability to find open ice, his lightning-quick release, his unparalleled one-timer. These attributes, however, are difficult to prove in any concrete way and are meaningless to somebody who doesn't understand the game of hockey. But there is another way to answer the question of how good Hull was, and that is to talk numbers. Factually speaking, Hull was a great hockey player because he scored 741 career goals, which places him third on the NHL all-time goal-scoring list.

The ability of numbers to succinctly and accurately describe a player's skills, or any given situation, for that matter, has created a language unto itself within the sports world. A number represents a benchmark by which all arguments about the quality of a player are eased. Think 500 goals, 1000 points, 50 goals in 50 games or 100 shutouts. With nothing more than a few digits, hockey fans are confident they can understand the merit of any player or the significance of any event. Numbers also describe the greatest moments and achievements in the game: 50 in 39, 1851, 92, +128. The beauty of these numbers is their representation of facts—these values have inherent objectivity. Hence, more measures are being traced, recorded, discussed and analyzed now, in the 21st century, than during any other time in history. No longer are statistics simply tracked. Instead, they're often run through the proverbial wringer by mathematicians and stats junkies, producing ever more complex—but valuable—ways of measuring and explaining the various games from which they're derived.

But the mainstream acceptance of advanced statistics in sports didn't happen overnight. Although the worlds of sports and numbers are closely intertwined, it's been an uphill battle, and some sports have fared far better than others in the war. Today, through the use of numbers, a small clique of dedicated hockey fans spend their time trying to expand and improve upon the methods we use to explain the game. But how did we get here, and where are we going? And most importantly, what does the statistical analysis of hockey mean to the average hockey fan?

Going Back in Time

Chronology dictates that any investigation into our fascination with sports, numbers and statistics has to begin with baseball. Alan Schwarz's seminal book, *The Numbers Game*, has much to say on the subject. According to Schwarz, it all started with a man by the name of Henry Chadwick, the "father of baseball." Chadwick, an Englishman and cricket fan who became obsessed with baseball after moving to the United States in 1836, was also an impassioned sportswriter and a pioneer in the field of sports journalism—a position that he first helped define during his post at the *New York Clipper*. Chadwick wrote about baseball as a gentleman's game and also pointed out the gambling problems it caused among its fans and players. Chadwick's interest in the sport was deeper than the game itself, though, and after 22 years in the

U.S., he was of the belief that the numbers under-lying baseball could offer valuable insights into players' actual (as opposed to perceived) abilities. But from the outset, Chadwick faced an obstacle: in 1858, such baseball statistics didn't exist.

However, with a bit of ambition and a conve-nient platform at the *Clipper*, Chadwick devel-oped the first "scoring" system for baseball statistics. This system involved a large grid into which he recorded the results of every event for every player in every game. No longer was an out (or "hand lost" in the parlance of the times) simply an out, but it was a strike out, foul out or some other measure codified by a letter and filled into a square on Chadwick's grid. After a baseball game was "scored," the results were tabulated and displayed in a box score—another idea of Chadwick's—and printed in the newspaper. He felt that the box score, which he adapted from his native land's game of cricket, provided a better context for the results of baseball games.

Chadwick, though, had more grandiose plans for his recorded statistics than the box score. His scor-ing system allowed him to track players not only game to game, but over an entire season—a giant leap in terms of establishing the relative values of baseball players, because one measure of talent is consistency, something that looking at individual game data might mask. But, while the concept of league leaders was born, Chadwick faced a problem in that players didn't always participate in an equal number of games. To counter this, he looked at statistics in terms of rates. Thus, batting average and earned run average came into existence, two metrics we continue to use to this day. In the 1861 edition of *Dime Base-Ball Player*, Chadwick's annual baseball publication, the season totals of a variety of statistics from five baseball teams were published for the first time.

Of course, the logistics of recording and maintaining statistics was extremely difficult with the limited technology available in the mid- to late 1800s and early 1900s. It isn't difficult to understand why this problem resulted in embarrassing situations for baseball officials. Discrepancies between statistics caused numerous controversies when records were broken (or not) and awards were handed out to players who many thought didn't deserve them. Avid baseball fan Al Munro Elias, along with his brother Walter, felt these unfortunate drawbacks needed fixing, and that they were the pair to provide the solution.

The Eliases started recording their own statistics around 1913, with the goal of creating a standard for the practice. At first they had difficulty finding customers for their service, but caught a break in

1916 by convincing a New York newspaper to publish the daily leaders in various baseball statistics. What set the Eliases apart was their uncanny ability to provide up-to-date stats, something newspapers of the day coveted. The idea caught on, and before long, the brothers were providing baseball statistics for hundreds of newspapers. In 1918, they became the official statistics provider of Major League Baseball's National League.

Today, the Elias Sports Bureau is the official statistical service for eight leagues around the world, including the NHL. Al and Walter Elias were successful because they understood that the numbers behind sports were compelling to fans. The brothers also realized that not just any numbers would suffice—the statistics had to be real and true. In other words, the statistics had to be *official*. Thus, the Eliases were able to fill a void by providing a service meant to solve old arguments, not start new ones.

Most sports fans were satisfied with reading and reviewing the official statistics provided by guys like the Elias brothers and published in daily newspapers and annual magazines, but George Lindsey understood that these numbers held even more untapped power. Born and raised in Toronto, Ontario, Lindsey grew up a hockey fan before becoming a military strategist, tasked with stopping the Russian threat of the 1950s from sending bombers through the east coast of Canada. Lindsey's position was reliant on data and the use of numbers to determine the best strategies to follow in protecting his fellow Canadians. The objective of his job was altruistic, but analyzing the strategies of how to stop a nonexistent threat could only occupy so much time. As a result, Lindsey became enamored with sports statistics and began trying to "figure out" the game of baseball.

In *The Numbers Game*, Schwarz describes Lindsey's attempts to answer the questions concerning the strategies of the sport. Lindsey didn't care to argue whether Ted Williams was a good hitter—that much was discernible from individual statistics that were already published. Rather, Lindsey was more interested in questions such as how much a batter's average was affected when he faced a left-handed pitcher versus a right-handed one. Or, how many runs was a team expected to score with the bases loaded and two out? In other words, to Lindsey the statistics weren't the end, but instead the means; they were data which, when plugged into fancy formulae, could help determine the best methods of winning the game.

The results of Lindsey's research, which relied on some 1200 innings of meticulous scoring by

Lindsey and his father, were published in three academic articles in the late 1950s and early 1960s. These articles dealt with questions that had plagued Lindsey, such as the aforementioned left-handed/right-handed platoon splits (he found out there is a significant difference), as well as how much variation was inherent in a player's batting average (he discovered there was quite a bit). Lindsey also calculated the probabilities of winning a baseball game based on how big a team's lead was and which inning the game was in. But his magnum opus was an eight-by-three matrix that determined the expected runs scored for each base runner/out combination. For example, with one out and runners on first and second, a team was expected to score, on average, 0.94 runs. With the bases loaded and two outs, 0.82 runs.

Lindsey's grid could be used to answer a number of tactical questions that arose in the course of a ball game, such as whether a team should bunt or steal. Yet despite the strategic importance of Lindsey's work, the baseball world hardly noticed it. Schwarz writes, "This new analysis did not shake baseball; it caused nary a tremor. No teams contacted Lindsey. No journalists wrote a word." Indeed, Lindsey's pioneering work in applying sports statistics to sports strategies remains unnoticed still—as typing his name into Google or Wikipedia will quickly reveal. But as the sports world continued its transition from hobby to business in the latter half of the 20th century, it did build—however unknowingly—upon the foundation that Lindsey helped establish.

Through gate receipts, concessions, souvenirs and minor marketing agreements, owning a sports franchise always provided a source of income for the team owner. But as televisions became more and more common in the living rooms of North Americans, savvy owners realized this was the start of something much bigger in terms of revenue. The 1950s saw many sports broadcasting milestones, including the first-ever public broadcast of *Hockey Night in Canada* in 1952, as well as the first televised pre-Super Bowl NFL Championship in 1958. Televised sporting events had the effect of widening the market for a local team, as well as adding a layer of personality to the game that radio couldn't provide. TV also created a completely new revenue stream: television rights. Corporate entities such as Imperial Oil, sponsors of the first *HNIC* broadcast, clamored over each other with sponsorship dollars at the ready.

Economic principles dictate that investment money will flow to where it can get the best return (for a given risk, of course). As professional sports grew into a multimillion-dollar industry through the 1950s, '60s and '70s, thanks in no small part to television, it was only natural that smart business people began to see sports teams as part of their investment strategies. Along with these new dollars came a corporate mentality and a penchant for minimizing costs and maximizing revenues. However, thanks to William Edwards Deming, the world of big business came to understand that it could achieve its goals through the use of statistics.

Deming was influential in the business sector because of his work in Japan's auto industry in the 1950s. Trained as a statistician, Deming worked with a special task force during World War II called the American War Standards. Their duty was to teach statistical process control (SPC) to manufacturing workers producing wartime goods, with the goal of increasing quality and efficiency. SPC became passé in America soon after the war, but Japan, mired in reconstruction, realized that Deming and his statistical methods for optimization were godsends. Japanese industry, particularly the automakers, followed Deming's advice, using statistics to strive to constantly improve quality, and Japan slowly became a manufacturing powerhouse. The rise of companies like Toyota and Honda (and the fall of their Detroit counterparts) owe much to Deming and his work.

But most importantly, Deming proved to the business world that it could garner practical, sound conclusions from statistical analysis. Many statistical approaches to improving processes and management built upon his work: Kaizen, Six Sigma, Total Quality Management, the Toyota Production System and many more. Thus, while sports evolved into a more business-oriented domain, it was only natural that clever owner-ship mimicked strategies employed by some of the most successful corporations on the planet. The Oakland A's baseball team experimented with these ideas when they hired Sandy Alderson as general manager of the team in 1982.

Alderson wasn't a baseball guy. In fact, he was first hired by Oakland as a legal consultant. He was an outsider. But what Alderson had going for him was a sharp, open mind. He may not have played baseball in a professional capacity like the majority of general managers, but he had a firm grasp of sound business practices. He understood that his job as general manager was to win games for the Athletics ownership, and he appreciated that analytics could help him do that.

Proving his faith in statistical analysis, Alderson commissioned a series of studies to determine which baseball statistics correlated most strongly with scoring runs, and, hence, winning. When he received the results, he set about building his team accordingly. The studies indicated that on-base percentage (OBP) was a good predictor of runs, and over the next 10 years of his tenure, Alderson's drafts, trades and free-agent signings reflected this newfound philosophy that was spawned from a single metric. With it came great success; the Oakland Athletics won their division four times between 1988 and 1992, and the American League pennant three times.

Alderson's hiring showed the sports community that it wasn't necessary to be a former player in order to run a team. By using business principles to guide decisions—that is, decisions based on data—success was possible. Of course, like any industry, professional sports have been slow to adapt, and few teams are willing to dismiss the "old boys club" and introduce a new way of doing business. As Deming discovered outside Japan after World War II, the status quo—for many—was always safer. Alderson may have taken a small step for sports, but he took a giant leap for a certain kind of man. Beyond proving the value of statistical analysis, Alderson showed outsider analysts that their work was relevant and there were opportunities in their field. This was great news for *the* ultimate outsider.

Bill James' baseball career ended before it really began, thanks to a childhood skill set that Schwarz describes as "distressingly unathletic." But James' inability to play the sport didn't diminish his passion for it, and James fulfilled his baseball obsession through statistics. From a young age, collecting and analyzing baseball cards, through to his high school years, during which he spent every waking minute manipulating statistics, it was clear to James why he was put on Earth.

After graduating from the University of Kansas with degrees in English and economics, followed by a one-year stint in the military, James returned to small-town Kansas and took a job as a night watchman for a canned goods company. The year was 1977, the pay was low and the work was mundane, but it afforded him the commodity he needed most: time. Thanks to the low crime rate associated with baked beans, James spent his time on duty computing advanced statistics by hand (he had no access to computers), and then using the data he produced as material for essays. But what set James apart from other number junkies were his incredible insights into the game as well as his ability to articulate them. He challenged conventional wisdom by looking at it through a statistical lens, and then explained it in ways that baseball fans could understand.

James decided to share his work with the public right away, and in 1977, he advertised his first *Baseball Abstract* in *The Sporting News* at a price of $3.50 a copy. He sold 70 issues. Rather than seeing this as a failure, James saw it as an achievement—there was an audience for this stuff! He persevered, producing his *Abstracts* for small audiences, until 1981. That year, he was profiled in *Sports Illustrated*, thanks to a connected fan of James', freelance journalist Dan Okrent. The article propelled James to sign a book deal with Ballantine, who published *The Baseball Abstract* from 1982 until 1988.

The irony is that despite his large following during the Ballantine years—some 150,000 readers—his clarity of argument and the obvious relevance of his work to decision-makers running professional baseball teams, James remained an outsider. In fact, he may be personally responsible for the dichotomy that developed between "numbers nerds" and "guys who actually played the game." Baseball insiders found it insulting that their assumptions might be wrong or that their eyes might deceive them. But as Schwarz says in *The Numbers Game*, "The naked eye cannot tell the difference between an average

(.275) and good (.300) hitter—just a hit every two weeks over the course of a season—without looking at the numbers." But nobody, especially those in high-level positions, likes being told they're off the mark.

James remained a successful outsider for many years, continuing to analyze and write about baseball in a variety of capacities, as well as influencing a new generation of intense baseball analysts. Nary a "sabermetrically" (a term coined by James, derived from SABR, the Society for American Baseball Research) inclined writer would exclude James from their list of influences. He published more than 20 books, but it wasn't until 2003 that he hit the ultimate jackpot. Inevitably, baseball ownership began to look at statistical efficiency to win. After 25 years of viewing baseball from the outside, James was hired by the Boston Red Sox as a special adviser. He was finally an insider. With the Red Sox, James was part of a management team that won two World Series in four years, helping to unify the paradigms of "numbers" versus "experience and gut feeling." James' work was so influential that it eventually transcended the green grass of the diamond, extending to the hardwood, the gridiron and yes, the rink.

Hitting the Ice

It was after reading James' 2002 book, *Win Shares*, that Alan Ryder had his "a-ha!" moment. James first introduced Win Shares in 2001, and followed it up with the book of the same name a year later. Win Shares was a new metric that translated a baseball player's statistics into a single number, which could then be compared across players, teams and eras. It was simple and elegant and, more importantly to Ryder, it could be applied to hockey. With little fanfare he put his mind to work, and after six months of gestation, produced his Player Contribution system. Ryder published his methodology and its results in an 80-page paper and posted it on his website. In 2004, the site had exactly 217 unique visitors.

Ryder didn't play a whole lot of ice hockey as a kid, thanks to "gifted hands but really bad feet." Growing up near Toronto, Ontario, however, ensured that he developed—at the very least—a love for hockey, and to this day his veins bleed the blue and white of the Maple Leafs. Although he lacked the necessary skills needed to play hockey, Ryder's prowess in statistics was evident at an early age. With a pen and paper in his hands, Ryder would sit in front of the television and "score" the game. He wasn't particularly tantalized by simple metrics such as goals and assists, but instead recorded and analyzed far more interesting things such as how often a defensive oversight resulted in a goal against. It was tedious, but it was also indicative of his affection for the sport and his devotion to understanding it on another level. Unfortunately, those were tough times for a hockey fan of Ryder's ilk because both the NHL's data collection and the Maple Leafs stunk. But Toronto was discovering a new love—the Blue Jays. This shift led Ryder into the loving arms of baseball, its excess of statistics and the work of Bill James.

Ryder appreciated James' ability to challenge the conventional wisdom of baseball by backing up assertions with statistics. It was a rough go at first—Ryder was a diehard hockey fan, after all—but James had no shortage of work for him to comb through and learn from. Although the dynamics of hockey and baseball are miles apart, Ryder understood that the principles James had developed and the foundation that he had laid were directly applicable to hockey. Ryder needed only to determine the methods. The first seeds of hockey analysis were planted...

The lack of an official home team didn't matter to Fredericton, New Brunswick, native Iain Fyffe. Self-confessed "terrible skater" and hockey fan Fyffe was instead wrapped up in his own ideas of how to read the stats pages of the news-paper just a bit differently than everyone else. A Maritimer through and through, Fyffe has lived in his hometown for over 30 years, all the while enjoying Canada's game from the prover-bial sidelines—with the exception of passing the puck around a bit during a few road-hockey games in the driveway. When not making these admittedly misguided attempts at improving his hockey skills, Fyffe was inside cheering for the Habs every Saturday night. This was simply carry-ing on a family tradition—many of Fyffe's child-hood memories include watching Montréal games with his father, a lifelong Canadiens fan.

For Fyffe, one of those cold New Brunswick winters stands out more than the others—that of 1988–89, one of the many glory years for the Canadiens. That Christmas, Fyffe's family pur-chased an NHL handbook, and at 13 years of age, Fyffe discovered that although he was untalented on the ice (and in the driveway), his true hockey sensibility came in the form of an ability to ana-lyze the game's statistics in ways that others weren't familiar with. Noticing in his handbook that players on the good teams tended to also have good plus-minus ratings, and vice versa for players on bad teams, Fyffe realized that a team's performance has a noticeable effect on each indi-vidual player's plus-minus rating. As a young teen, he created a simple method to produce an adjusted plus-minus rating to account for how a team's overall skill ended up affecting this player stat. His method was to calculate the team's average plus-minus rating for forwards and defensemen per game, and then subtract it from each player's plus-minus rating per game. Toiling away with his pencil poised and memories of many games past, Fyffe saw the necessity of considering that since a team had a different number of forwards and defensemen, these two groups of players had to have different plus-minus averages, which were dependent on a player's ice time— a statistic that wasn't even tracked at the end of the 1980s. No matter for Fyffe—he was hooked on the idea that not everything in hockey stats was what it first seemed. He continued with his work, later realizing how far he had developed his abilities when, after reading the *Hockey Compendium* by pro hockey writers Jeff Klein and Karl-Eric Reif, he noticed that they failed to address the need to consider ice time when looking at a player's plus-minus rating—a concept he had grasped at the age of 13.

Fyffe continues to contribute to the largely underground group of hockey statisticians who doggedly pursue this infinitely interesting topic, which is still in its infancy. Perhaps because of this, Fyffe, while still a diehard Habs fan, also pledges his player devotions to skaters like Martin St. Louis, whom Fyffe considers an underrated player because of his small size—a fitting analogy for the greatly undervalued world Fyffe has dedicated much of his life to.

Canadians, however, aren't the only ones interested in the still-developing world of hockey stats analysis. Ken Kryzwicki of the Windy City is much like his counterparts from the Great White North. Hockey has been a permanent fixture in Kryzwicki's life, whether that included a stick to the face, a shiner to beat all shiners or a puck to the nose. These literal run-ins might have been enough to turn any other naturally self-preserving individual away from the game, but not Kryzwicki. A fan of hockey since he could understand the words "Chicago" and "Blackhawks," Kryzwicki considers himself a lifelong supporter of the 'Hawks, and thanks to his great uncle, who had season tickets at Chicago Stadium during Kryzwicki's youth, he was able to attend game after game, cheering on his hometown team and favorite player Keith Magnuson. Next to wearing a Blackhawks jersey and skating around on a homemade rink every winter with a friend who, without fail, always donned a North Stars jersey, the late Magnuson was at the centre of one of Kryzwicki's most prominent hockey memories: a slap shot Magnuson took to the jaw, courtesy of Brad Park. Perhaps feeling a special kinship with Magnuson because of the facial-injury element, Kryzwicki also counts his own broken nose among his most memorable hockey moments. With his father and girlfriend in the stands, neither of whom had ever met the other, Kryzwicki took a clearing shot to the face. While being helped off the ice by teammates, Kryzwicki's top two fans rushed down to check on him, at which point he introduced them and was taken to the nearest emergency room to get stitched up.

Kryzwicki, who stopped playing hockey in amateur leagues as a child and then began again as an adult in a men's league, also uses his interest in hockey in a more cerebral manner that poses little risk of bloodshed on the ice. A math major in university and in grad school, Kryzwicki was first intrigued by the possibilities of hockey statistical analysis when he used a bit of hockey data for a school project. Later, in his professional life building statistical models, Kryzwicki realized that what he had learned at school and on the job translated well into the analysis of hockey data. His first project was a goalie analysis in 1998, and he was immediately hooked on the untapped potential of what NHL data could tell fans.

Although the work was difficult to sell through freelancing, Kryzwicki didn't mind doing the analyses for his own enjoyment, and his initial passing interest has turned into much more than that, bringing him to where he is today in the hockey statistical analysis community. And upcoming for Kryzwicki is one of his most important projects to date: teaching his son to skate—while both father and son wear helmets with visors, of course.

Following their passion for what they believed was (and is) a field worth much more intense scrutiny than is currently given to it, the work of Ryder, Fyffe and Kryzwicki has not been lost on a newer generation of analysts who have seen and appreciated the value of their efforts. One such person is Chris Boersma, a Vancouverite for life in more ways than one. Born and raised in the West Coast's most famous metropolis, Boersma is a staunch supporter of the Vancouver Canucks. Building on his fan loyalty and a penchant for statistical analysis, Boersma has made his mark in this figurative arena, rather than in the literal one.

Admitting a lack of enthusiasm for picking up a hockey stick himself, what NHL players are doing with theirs is an entirely different story. Boersma is the webmaster and blogger behind the hockey analysis website Hockey Numbers, but his interest in the topic was slow to develop. The first prickling of curiosity in stats itself came in high school, when Boersma was forced to suffer through a small unit on statistics. But he soon discovered that he wasn't suffering at all and was diving right in, taking what he had learned in class and applying key principles to any and all data he could get his hands on. Eventually—and voluntarily—taking a course on nonlinear regression, Boersma knew he had found his calling, and also, around the same time, discovered the website that helped guide him in applying his considerable talent to hockey stats: Ryder's hockeyanalytics.com. A young person in this field of study, the possibilities for future analyses seemed endless, and Ryder's Player Contribution and shot quality analysis articles propelled Boersma into looking at his beloved Vancouver Canucks in an entirely new light.

Unable to name a favorite player on his team of choice, Boersma instead prefers to take players he thinks stand out from others on the Canucks roster and make individual case studies of them. In doing so, he has seen the overlooked talent in players who have gotten traded or not re-signed, and therefore wonders what could have been had their statistics been studied more closely. For example, defenseman Tomas Mojzis played for the

Canucks in the 2005–06 season, and although he only skated in seven games, Mojzis never allowed a goal against, except for one on a five-on-three penalty kill. Traded at the deadline of that season, Mojzis has disappeared into relative obscurity and now plays for the Houston Aeros, a Minnesota Wild affiliate. Boersma still ponders whether this largely forgotten player would have turned into a good defenseman in the NHL if Vancouver been more aware of his remarkable record in the position.

Boersma's tracking of players like Mojzis is evident again in his curiosity surrounding Josh Green, a left-winger who played for the Canucks in the 2006–07 season. Green was the number one penalty killer in the league that year, and by quite a large margin. Vancouver didn't re-sign Green at the end of the season, though, and he took off to play for a team in an entirely different league and country: the Red Bulls Salzburg, an Austrian club. Boersma has wondered since then, if given another chance in the NHL, would Green have kept up his awesome performance, or would he have descended into the mediocrity otherwise known as the league average? Boersma might yet have his chance to find out because Green was signed as a free agent with the Anaheim Ducks in 2008.

In monitoring players such as Mojzis and Green, Boersma has shown his knack for picking out the unusual in what appears to be the usual. This ability reflects his belief that asking questions about which statistics are meaningful is the key to relevant analysis, rather than choosing to look at stats whose dicey value produces nothing more than the metaphorical equivalent of picking a number from a hat. The challenge lies in figuring out which stats are the important ones, using those numbers to produce something worthwhile and then convincing the skeptics of the relevance of hockey analysis for everyone from the fans to the players to the GMs of both the "best" and the "worst" teams in the NHL.

Cautious Optimism

The quartet of Ryder, Fyffe, Kryzwicki and Boersma stand among a small group at the forefront of the statistical analysis of hockey. And although their work is largely unknown outside their inner circle, these men are slowly but surely continuing to dig through their data, shaping their spreadsheets and finessing their formulae with the hope of understanding hockey better than we do today. Their efforts are not unlike the humble beginnings of Henry Chadwick, many years ago.

Despite their varied backgrounds, these hockey analysts share some of the lessons learned from the insider-versus-outsider struggles first experienced in the baseball world. "This discipline is not meant to replace traditional methods," explains Kryzwicki, "rather to enhance them. It can help corroborate or debunk a hunch or commonly held belief." But even though they have confidence that their work is relevant, these men realize there is no point being militant about their methods because the old guard just won't get it. "There are some people that if they don't know, you can't tell them. They'll never be convinced, because they've decided that statistical analysis is useless, and no amount of evidence will convince them," says Fyffe. "Those people aren't the audience, and trying to make them the audience is futile."

Part of their passive attitude exists because these analysts understand that baseball and hockey are completely different games, and the dynamic nature of hockey makes it harder put numbers on the game. This difference has put hockey well behind baseball in terms of statistical understanding. "Baseball analysis has led the way because it is a game of a limited number of states," Ryder explains. "It can be modeled accurately in discrete steps. This is not the case with hockey. Hockey is fluid and can only be modeled approximately." Boersma agrees, stating that

"Hockey might be the hardest sport to analyze. The parts of the game that are critical to a team's success—like battles along the boards and puck movement—cannot be measured."

No one can say, however, that the preliminary efforts of today's hockey analysts have been in vain. It's clear to these armchair analysts that what we currently have in terms of metrics isn't going to cut it and can easily be improved upon. "Hockey is awash with meaningless and, even worse, misleading statistics," Ryder sighs. He presents the goaltender's win statistic as an example. "Someone decided to borrow this from baseball. But a typical team leans heavily on one goaltender, which makes the results of the team and goalie indistinguishable." Rather than simply complaining about what we have to work with, Ryder has replaced the bad with good, developing a much better measure of netminder performance: Shot Quality Neutral Save Percentage.

The NHL has not helped matters, though. The ease with which baseball can be described by numbers alone, combined with the insatiable appetite that its fans have for statistics, has forced Major League Baseball to be on the cutting edge of data tracking. Not so for data-hungry hockey fans. In fact, many analysts don't see hockey analysis progressing much further if the NHL doesn't pick up the slack. "If the data quality and elements get better, [hockey analysis] could become more mainstream," Kryzwicki explains. He knows as well as anyone the limitations of the current catalog of statistics offered by professional hockey. Kryzwicki has spent years trying to develop a good draft model, even getting some interest from a scouting service, but he has never been able to complete his work. He knew what he wanted and how to do it, but "all I was missing was the proper data."

Boersma considers this the main problem facing hockey analysts. Where does he see the field in 10 years? "Not much further. While each individual analyst will get better at what they do, they'll still be limited by the information in the scoring reports. Only the NHL has the ability to increase the data."

Fyffe isn't so cynical. Recently drawn from an analytical slumber to write for the newly launched Puck Prospectus website, he sees the progress of hockey analysis as slow but typical. Fyffe points out how long it took rigorous baseball analysis to get a toehold despite the fact that "baseball has mountains of statistical information." He says the reception of Puck Prospectus has been very good and believes that the NHL is moving in the right direction with respect to their data collection and distribution. "Before 1967, what do we have in a skater's record? Games played, goals, assists and penalty minutes. That's not much to work with. The introduction of real-time stats, allowing actual ice-time numbers, among other things, was a big step." He holds out hope for headway within the decade.

Despite the complaints and annoyances, this small sample of hockey analysts agrees that they're going to maintain the course. "A long time ago, I learned that if I'm doing something, I should first make sure I enjoy what I am doing," says Boersma. And playing with hockey data is exactly such a thing. Boersma spends his spare minutes writing for his weblog, Hockey Numbers, complete with a database filled with unique statistics. "There are very few places you can find interesting statistical projects that can be analyzed every year and that produce such dramatically different results. Hockey's also fun to watch."

Fyffe is going to continue to dig into the data under a variety of guises. Foremost is the website, for which he was recruited, that is probably one of the most likely vehicles to bust this field into the mainstream. But he won't neglect the Hockey Analysis Group, known as HAG, an old-school Yahoo! newsgroup he founded years ago that now boasts hundreds of members. "I don't harbor any illusions that my work will revolutionize the way NHL teams look at their players or anything like that. I just know there is quite a sizable number of people who are interested in this stuff, so I like to share it with them."

For Kryzwicki, there remains a glimmer of hope that he can parlay his extensive knowledge into some freelance work for a professional team. Although there has been interest in a few of his projects, nothing concrete has materialized. But that's not going to slow him down. "My original motivation was freelance work, but I realize that probably isn't going to happen. I'll keep at it because it is interesting, challenging and," he says with a gulp, "fun." Get Kryzwicki talking about what he has up his sleeve and his enthusiasm for analysis and what's next comes out in spades. "I'd love to build that draft model. And I'm interested to know the relationship between fighting and a goal being scored in the next few minutes." Fine-tuning his work on NHL career curves is also on the menu, "And, as in prior seasons, I'll be collecting the play-by-play data and parsing it out. Once the grueling part of cleansing and auditing is finished, I will share it with HAG. If I need to recalibrate my shot quality model, I will do that as well."

Ryder, likely the most famous name among the inner circle of objective hockey analysts, continues to write a semi-regular article for the *Globe and Mail*, geared toward intelligent and analytic readers. Even though he's pioneered much of the work in the field of hockey analysis and has achieved a modicum of fame, Ryder maintains he's just a hockey fan at heart. "All that distinguishes me from the average fan is my statistical training and my willingness to use it." The target of said training will continue to be a precise measurement of defense, something Ryder considers to be the least understood aspect of the game of hockey. His excitement for such analysis hasn't waned in the least. "I feel a bit like the guy who just invented the ruler and runs around measuring stuff."

Back to the Ballpark

After 150 years of scrutiny, there are few stones that baseball analysts have left unturned. But there remains one obvious holdout—one great, big, pervasive stone. Defense. In *The Numbers Game*, Schwarz refers to a concise measure of defense as baseball's "holy grail." Despite its importance—half of each baseball game is played on defense, after all—little progress has been made in a century and a half of measurement, and not for lack of trying.

Some of the biggest names in the field have stepped up to the plate, with little success. Chadwick used a variation of fielding percentage in the 19th century, despite knowing that it was, for the most part, useless. Other baseball statisticians who tried to tie a number to defense include Pete Palmer, John Dewan and Bill James.

The reason for failure, according to Schwarz, is that all the methodologies rely on "the same specious input: putouts, assists and errors." But these advanced metrics are nothing more than the final event in a complex process that starts when the batter makes contact with the ball. Nowhere is the quality of that contact mentioned. Nor is the fielder's "jump" or positioning taken into account. In other words, the data we have can't quite capture the essence of what we are trying to measure.

But what's discouraging for baseball is encouraging for hockey. There are similarities between defense in America's favorite pastime and hockey. Both are dynamic and rely on factors that aren't always conducive to calculation. But while defense in baseball has thus far relied on three simple statistics, hockey has a catalog of metrics available, and that catalog is growing, whereas baseball's is not.

Fortunately, after a century and a half, there's no chance that baseball analysts are going to allow the defense puzzle to go unsolved. Sabermetricians will continue to pound away at a solution. And thanks to the similarities with hockey, the solutions, be they mathematical or technological, are bound to flow between the two sports. So, even though the "when" question can be answered with a slightly unsatisfying "eventually," there still remains the question of "why." Why do hundreds of brilliant minds insist on turning our beloved sports into mathematical exercises? Why did statistical analysis creep from baseball to hockey, and what insights can it offer the average fan? Simply: why bother with it at all?

Chapter Two

Why Bother With Hockeynomics?

Arguing like a Professional

If hockey is one of our favorite pastimes, then arguing about hockey probably comes in a close second on the list of a sports fan's top activities. Most fans can recall at some point in their lives sitting on the couch having a beer or three, discussing the merits of this or that player. Discussions can be intense, especially if the argument involves the players or team of a fan's home city. The nice thing for regular folk, though, is that in the end, there's nothing riding on the debate except pride. But what happens if it's not only your pride but also your job that is on the line?

The job of an NHL general manager is to win games. In order to do that, the general manager has to assemble a team consisting of the best possible players. However, the GM faces a constraint—payroll. In days of yore, payroll was determined by a team's ownership, with an unlimited upper bound and a lower bound determined by the league's "minimum wage." But since the 2004 NHL lockout, the upper limit to payroll has been established by a salary cap. Essentially, this cap tightens the financial constraint on the GMs, making the job of team construction more difficult. Teams that previously had payrolls higher than the salary cap now have fewer resources to divvy up among the same number of players; teams that were under the cap now face increased efficiency in player spending, making it more difficult to find those diamonds in the rough.

The problem of payroll allocation is amplified when you examine the near-infinite ways payroll can be divided among the players of a team. Certain distributions of money can be ruled out. For instance, spending most of the payroll on a star forward trio and apportioning the rest to marginal players making the minimum wage is no way to win a championship—nor is spending $50 million on the genetically engineered love child of Dominik Hasek and Patrick Roy, only to rely on the equivalent of a double-A bantam team to score goals. Yet in between the extremes, there is a multitude of payroll allotments.

So let's get you up off the couch, into your best suit and off to a parallel universe where you are the GM of an NHL franchise. It's the 2007 off-season, and as far as your team is concerned, you're in a pretty good place. Your team snuck into the playoffs by three points, but was then eliminated in the first round by the team that went on to win the Stanley Cup. The core of your team has remained intact, less one spot. Soothsayers and experts alike are predicting that the next season will be similar to the last one—with a few bounces you'll be in the hunt for a playoff spot come April. All you have to do is fill one more roster spot. Your team needs a forward. No problem.

You've been informed that the owner of your team has authorized full use of available salary-cap space, leaving you with $6 million and change to sign a player. However, before you go out and sign the most expensive free-agent forward your budget allows, your boss—the owner of the team—reminds you that every penny you spend on this forward comes right out of his pocket. In fact, he offers you a deal as an incentive to remain as frugal as possible in your selection. For every dollar you remain under the salary cap, you'll get a $0.25 bonus. The catch is that you absolutely have to make the playoffs. History has proven that there is quite a bit of luck involved in winning the Stanley Cup—a hot goalie, overachieving special teams—and the owner understands that. But you have to at least give your team that chance to win, not to mention line the pockets of the owner with the gate receipts from post-season games. Bottom line: if your team doesn't make the playoffs, you're out of a job.

The problem at the heart of this thought experiment is how to get the best player possible without spending any more money than necessary. This quandary arises because resources surrounding a hockey team and the game itself are limited. Teams have a budget and thus limited funds. The size of a team roster is restricted to 23 players. A team can only field six skaters at any time. There are only 60 minutes in a hockey game. Yet, how money, roster positions, linemates and ice time (as well as many other factors) are allocated determines whether or not a team wins games, the owner makes money and you keep your job. It's a complicated relational matrix, and it's hard to imagine how any person could arrive at the optimal solution. Unfortunately, some poor suckers are cursed with having to do just this, and their livelihood depends on it. In our little role-playing experiment, you're one such sucker.

So you've got your assignment and your budget. Let's look at the top 15 forwards from 2006–07.

For the purpose of this experiment, the year is irrelevant. The 2006–07 season is as good as any, since it has complete data and also allows for hindsight. Following are the top forwards arranged by goals scored. Why goals? Because hockey is all about scoring goals. Many other factors come into play in the course of a game or season, but the fact remains that if a team doesn't score, it will win exactly zero games. Besides that, the goals statistic is readily available and is relatable for even the most casual fan. Here are the top 15 forwards in the NHL from 2006–07:

Table 1						
Player	Team	Position	GP	G	A	P
Vincent Lecavalier	TBL	C	82	52	56	108
Dany Heatley	OTT	LW	82	50	55	105
Teemu Selanne	ANA	RW	82	48	46	94
Alex Ovechkin	WAS	LW	82	46	46	92
Marian Hossa	ATL	RW	82	43	57	100
Martin St. Louis	TBL	RW	82	43	59	102
Thomas Vanek	BUF	LW	82	43	41	84
Ilya Kovalchuk	ATL	LW	82	42	34	76
Simon Gagne	PHI	LW	76	41	27	68
Jason Blake	NYI	C	82	40	29	69
Jarome Iginla	CGY	RW	70	39	55	94
Olli Jokinen	FLA	C	82	39	52	91
Alexander Semin	WAS	LW	77	38	35	73
Chris Drury	BUF	C	77	37	32	69
Jonathan Cheechoo	SJS	RW	76	37	32	69

The list in Table 1 consists of great players, any of whom you'd love to fill a roster spot with. Unfortunately, most of these players are unavailable and are probably too expensive for you, even if you could tender them an offer. Instead, you'll have to select from unrestricted free agents (UFAs). Here is a list of the top 25 free-agent forwards from the 2007 off-season, again sorted by goals scored:

Table 2							
Player	Age	Team	Position	GP	G	A	P
Jason Blake	33	NYI	C	82	40	29	69
Chris Drury	30	BUF	C	77	37	32	69
Bill Guerin	36	2Tm	RW	77	36	20	56
Ryan Smyth	30	2Tm	LW	71	36	32	68
Joe Sakic	37	COL	C	82	36	64	100
Daniel Briere	29	BUF	C	81	32	63	95
Ray Whitney	34	CAR	LW	81	32	51	83
Brendan Shanahan	38	NYR	LW	67	29	33	62
Vyacheslav Kozlov	34	ATL	LW	81	28	52	80
Keith Tkachuk	34	2Tm	LW	79	27	31	58
Pavel Datsyuk	28	DET	C	79	27	60	87
Michael Nylander	34	NYR	C	79	26	57	83
Viktor Kozlov	31	NYI	C	81	25	26	51
Paul Kariya	32	NAS	LW	82	24	52	76
Dainius Zubrus	28	2Tm	C	79	24	36	60
Scott Hartnell	24	NAS	LW	64	22	17	39
Petr Sykora	30	EDM	RW	82	22	31	53
Mike Comrie	26	2Tm	C	65	20	25	45
Jeff O'Neill	30	TOR	RW	74	20	22	42

Table 2 cont.							
Player	Age	Team	Position	GP	G	A	P
Scott Gomez	27	NJD	C	72	13	47	60
Ladislav Nagy	27	2Tm	LW	80	12	43	55
Mike Johnson	32	MTL	RW	80	11	20	31
Michael Peca	32	TOR	C	35	4	11	15
Michal Handzus	29	CHI	C	8	3	5	8
Todd Bertuzzi	31	2Tm	RW	15	3	8	11

Only two of the players in the   (Jason Blake and Chris Drury) appear in the top 15 in the league in goals scored. Still, there are some great players here. With your job at risk on one hand and your bonus at risk on the other, who do you sign?

Rates Matter

Being as how goals are so vital to winning hockey games, attempting to sign the player you deem to be the best goal scorer makes a lot of sense. With 40 goals in the 2006–07 season, that player is Jason Blake, right? Maybe, maybe not. Look at the following two players:

Table 3			
	G	A	P
Player A	45	58	103
Player B	53	83	136

Which of the two is the better goal scorer? You might assume that since Player B has better counting statistics (his goal total is higher) than Player A, Player B is the better of the two. Let's look at Player A and B in a different light:

Table 4				
	GP	G	A	P
Player A	79	45	58	103
Player B	576	53	83	136

With that slight modification it becomes clear that Player A is the better player. Player B has more goals (and assists and points) than Player A, but Player A has played significantly fewer games than Player B. You see how this reasoning can serve you well as an NHL general manager when it is revealed that Player B shows the career line of Basil McRae, better known for fisticuffs than finesse, and Player A is 26-year-old Steve Yzerman from the 1991–92 season.

This idea may seem intuitive to a hockey fan, but it gets at the fundamental principle of rates versus counting statistics. It's difficult to determine the relative rank of two numbers without some concept of time. If someone tells you that they earn $1000 at their job, does that person mean $1000 annually or $1000 hourly? Compared to the earnings of the average Canadian, the first value is very low, whereas the second value is spectacularly large. The same concept can be applied to an NHL player's goals scored. A higher total doesn't necessarily make for a better player. Rates matter. Let's look at another example:

Table 5		
	GP	G
Player A	82	25
Player B	76	23

These two players are obviously similar. Player A has slightly more goals than Player B, but has also played in a few more games. And although not shown in the table, the goals-per-game rates of both players are identical. So which player is the more effective goal scorer? We can get closer to the answer if we dig a little deeper into the statistics. Here they are again:

Table 6			
	GP	G	ATOI
Player A	82	25	24
Player B	76	23	14

From this table we can see that Player A averages 24 minutes per game. Player B plays only 14 minutes per game. This is significant because 24 minutes is a ton of ice time for a forward. To get 24 minutes of ice time in a game, a forward has to take a regular shift on the first or second line as well as earn some playing time on special teams. On the other hand, a player can get 14 minutes of ice time in a game simply by taking a regular shift on the second or third line. The players are similar on a per-game level, but on a per-minute-of-ice-time basis, Player B is a much better goal scorer.

Peeking behind the curtain reveals that Player A is Brad Richards and the corresponding stats are from his 2006–07 season with the Tampa Bay Lightning. Player B is from the same season—Taylor Pyatt of the Vancouver Canucks. If you had an unlimited budget and tried to tell me that you'd rather have Pyatt on your team than Richards, I'd recommend you give your head a shake. Looking at their complete scoring lines in 2006–07, Richards is well ahead of Pyatt in assists and points and has half as many penalty minutes. Richards has also won a Stanley Cup, a Conn Smythe Trophy as the NHL playoff MVP and has played for Team Canada in the Olympics. Pyatt is an above-average power forward and a former fourth-round draft pick. Yet the dynamics of hockey are such that you can't field a team of Brad Richardses playing 24 minutes per game. There just isn't enough ice time to go around. You need to have players who soak up minutes while your stars are on the bench. Within that framework and from a pure goal-scoring-efficiency standpoint, it might be better to have Pyatt on your second or third line than Richards on your first. Once again, rates matter, and Pyatt scores more goals per minute of ice time. And goals are how you win hockey games.

This argument bears repeating. Goals are a function of talent and ice time; a player will score fewer goals the fewer minutes he plays, all things being equal. Therefore, if you want to pencil Richards in on your first line, it's important to realize that he is going to take ice time away from somebody else. If the player Richards replaces scores more goals per minute of ice time (like Pyatt), you're going to score fewer goals *as a team*. Put another way, Richards might be a better player than Pyatt, but much of Richards' value comes from his ability to play a lot of ice time in many different situations. If you only have 10 or 12 minutes of ice time to spare (a second- or third-line spot), you're probably better off with Pyatt than Richards. The statistics show that Pyatt might score more goals in that situation than Richards would.

We can now venture back into the confines of your corner office at the headquarters of the NHL team you've been hired to manage. Remember that you have the luxury of filling the roster spot with any forward—first, second, third or even fourth line. Thanks to this luxury, it may be most efficient to determine which player has the highest goal-scoring rate and slide him into the lineup where he fits best. Here's a list of the same free agents from Table 2, sorted by goals per minute of ice time:

Table 7			
Player	G	TOI(M)	G/Min
Bill Guerin	36	1309	0.028
Jason Blake	40	1488	0.027
Chris Drury	37	1446	0.026
Ryan Smyth	36	1472	0.024
Scott Hartnell	22	1006	0.022
Brendan Shanahan	29	1328	0.022
Joe Sakic	36	1655	0.022
Ray Whitney	32	1515	0.021
Daniel Briere	32	1564	0.020
Mike Comrie	20	991	0.020
Jeff O'Neill	20	1016	0.020
Keith Tkachuk	27	1382	0.020
Viktor Kozlov	25	1330	0.019
Michal Handzus	3	168	0.018
Pavel Datsyuk	27	1577	0.017
Vyacheslav Kozlov	28	1660	0.017
Michael Nylander	26	1610	0.016
Petr Sykora	22	1366	0.016
Dainius Zubrus	24	1540	0.016

Table 7 cont.			
Player	G	TOI(M)	G/Min
Paul Kariya	24	1671	0.014
Todd Bertuzzi	3	240	0.013
Scott Gomez	13	1363	0.010
Mike Johnson	11	1231	0.009
Ladislav Nagy	12	1386	0.009
Michael Peca	4	609	0.007

A cursory examination of this table imparts a couple of things. First, there is some shuffling of the order when the players are sorted by goals per minute rather than goals scored in a season. Second, the actual value that the goals-per-minute metric, or statistic, produces is, well, ludicrous. If during an argument you were to proclaim, "O'Neill is clearly a better goal scorer than Tkachuk, as his zero-point-oh-one-nine-six versus zero-point-oh-one-nine-FIVE goals per minute statistic shows," you're likely going to be met with some blank stares. The numbers lack context, and their small magnitude makes them cumbersome.

To solve this problem, we can make a slight adjustment to the metric. By multiplying goals per minute by 60, we obtain goals per 60 minutes. Sixty minutes is significant because it's the length of an NHL hockey game. This adjustment scales the metric into more familiar territory as well as adds some context. Goals per 60 minutes calculates how many goals a player would score if he played every minute of a game (theoretically, of course). Here are our 25 free agents again, this time sorted by goals scored per 60 minutes:

Player	G/60	Goal Rank	Diff.
Bill Guerin	1.65	3	+2
Jason Blake	1.61	1	-1
Chris Drury	1.54	2	-1
Ryan Smyth	1.47	4	+0
Scott Hartnell	1.31	16	+11
Brendan Shanahan	1.31	8	+2
Joe Sakic	1.31	5	-2
Ray Whitney	1.27	6	-2
Daniel Briere	1.23	7	-2
Mike Comrie	1.21	18	+8
Jeff O'Neill	1.18	19	+8
Keith Tkachuk	1.17	10	-2
Viktor Kozlov	1.13	13	+0
Michal Handzus	1.07	24	+10
Pavel Datsyuk	1.03	11	-4
Vyacheslav Kozlov	1.01	9	-7
Michael Nylander	0.97	12	-5
Petr Sykora	0.97	17	-1
Dainius Zubrus	0.93	14	-5
Paul Kariya	0.86	15	-5
Todd Bertuzzi	0.75	25	+4
Scott Gomez	0.57	20	-2
Mike Johnson	0.54	22	-1

Table 8

Table 8 cont.			
Player	G/60	Goal Rank	Diff.
Ladislav Nagy	0.52	21	-3
Michael Peca	0.39	23	-2

If you're going to use the goals-per-60-minutes metric to determine which player to sign, the most important change occurs at the top of the list. Bill Guerin is now the guy you want to go after, jumping up two spots, from third in goals in Table 2 to the top position in goals per 60 minutes. That's not much of a change, and looking at goals alone told us that Guerin could score. As a matter of fact, the top of the list changes very little. Blake drops from the top of the list to second place, and Drury drops from second in goals to third in goals per 60 minutes. Ryan Smyth doesn't move at all, placing fourth on both lists. There isn't anything disturbing about these results. Players who score a lot of goals are good, and good players tend to be efficient goal scorers.

In the fifth spot, we do see something compelling. Scott Hartnell jumps 11 spots, from 16th in goals into fifth place in goals per 60 minutes. Hartnell is a hard-nosed winger who holds the Nashville Predators' franchise record for career penalty minutes. He typically plays on the second or third line. In an absolute sense, he doesn't score many goals, yet his goal-scoring *rate* during the 2006–07 season was as good as Joe Sakic's. Getting production like that from someone down the depth chart is valuable. Remember, someone has to play on the second, third and fourth lines. Without looking at rates, Hartnell is overshadowed in this group of free agents.

Other movers and shakers are Mike Comrie and Jeff O'Neill, both jumping up eight spots between Table 2 and Table 8. The biggest loser is Vyacheslav Kozlov, who drops seven positions. Michal Handzus and Todd Bertuzzi were both limited by injuries to very few games played, which affected their goal totals. However, when we look at goal-scoring rates, Handzus moves right into the middle of the pack of free agents, while Bertuzzi continues to flounder near the bottom.

Regardless, you've got the information you need. Guerin is the most efficient goal scorer on a per-minute basis and, as such, is your free-agent target. This decision is easier to accept because he also scored a pile of goals during the 2006–07 season. I suppose it's time to contact the team attorney to draft up a contract offer. Or is it?

Goals Ain't Everything

I can sense the criticism associated with deter-mining a player's offensive abilities based on goals alone. From a young age, players and fans are told that an assist is as good as a goal. This attitude is supported by the fact that the most famous hockey player of all time—Wayne Gretzky—is regarded as a playmaker, despite his possession of nearly every goal-scoring record. As such, you'd be hard-pressed to convince a hockey fan that assists, and in turn total points, are irrelevant when discussing a player's scoring prowess. Perhaps as an NHL GM trying to win games as efficiently as possible, you should include goals *and* assists in your analysis? Here's our list of available free agents again:

Table 9				
Player	GP	G	A	P
Joe Sakic	82	36	64	100
Daniel Briere	81	32	63	95
Pavel Datsyuk	79	27	60	87
Ray Whitney	81	32	51	83
Michael Nylander	79	26	57	83
Vyacheslav Kozlov	81	28	52	80
Paul Kariya	82	24	52	76
Jason Blake	82	40	29	69
Chris Drury	77	37	32	69
Ryan Smyth	71	36	32	68
Brendan Shanahan	67	29	33	62
Dainius Zubrus	79	24	36	60
Scott Gomez	72	13	47	60
Keith Tkachuk	79	27	31	58
Bill Guerin	77	36	20	56

Table 9 cont.			
Player	GP	G	A	P
Ladislav Nagy	80	12	43	55
Petr Sykora	82	22	31	53
Viktor Kozlov	81	25	26	51
Mike Comrie	65	20	25	45
Jeff O'Neill	74	20	22	42
Scott Hartnell	64	22	17	39
Mike Johnson	80	11	20	31
Michael Peca	35	4	11	15
Todd Bertuzzi	15	3	8	11
Michal Handzus	8	3	5	8

That sure throws a wrench into the Guerin decision. When total points are used as the metric to determine the best player to sign, Sakic marches to the front of the pack. However, like total goals, total points don't tell you how *efficient* a player is at getting points. As was argued, valuable insights can be gained by using rates. Applying the same methodology as earlier (dividing points by minutes played), here are the free agents arranged by points per 60 minutes:

Table 10			
Player	P	TOI	P/60
Daniel Briere	95	1564	3.645
Joe Sakic	100	1655	3.625
Pavel Datsyuk	87	1577	3.310
Ray Whitney	83	1515	3.287

Table 10 cont.			
Player	P	TOI	P/60
Michael Nylander	83	1610	3.093
Vyacheslav Kozlov	80	1660	2.892
Chris Drury	69	1446	2.863
Michal Handzus	8	168	2.857
Brendan Shanahan	62	1328	2.801
Jason Blake	69	1488	2.782
Ryan Smyth	68	1472	2.772
Todd Bertuzzi	11	240	2.750
Paul Kariya	76	1671	2.729
Mike Comrie	45	991	2.725
Scott Gomez	60	1363	2.641
Bill Guerin	56	1309	2.567
Keith Tkachuk	58	1382	2.518
Jeff O'Neill	42	1016	2.480
Ladislav Nagy	55	1386	2.381
Dainius Zubrus	60	1540	2.338
Petr Sykora	53	1366	2.328
Scott Hartnell	39	1006	2.326
Viktor Kozlov	51	1330	2.301
Mike Johnson	31	1231	1.511
Michael Peca	15	609	1.478

This list looks much different than the list of free agents arranged by goals per 60 minutes in Table 8. Now you face a problem. You want to sign the best forward possible, yet two measures of a forward's offensive abilities—goals per 60 minutes and points per 60 minutes—give you completely different recommendations. At this point, you feel forced to make an entirely subjective personnel decision, which is what you are, ideally, trying to avoid. There has to be a better method.

The core of the problem is how to value an assist. No hockey purist would argue that assists are a useless statistic, so assists need to be included somewhere in the measure of a player's offensive capability. On the other hand, it is equally difficult to argue that assists and goals should be treated the same, which is what the statistic "points" tells us. One reason for this difficulty is that up to two assists are doled out per goal scored. From 1990 onwards, the NHL has averaged about 1.7 assists per goal. Another snag in the argument is that although a goal can be scored unassisted, a player cannot get an assist without a goal being scored (profound, I know). The differences in relative scarcity of goals and assists imply they should be valued differently. Fortunately, hockey analysts have a tool that does just that: Goals Created.

Goals Created has its roots in Runs Created, a statistic developed by baseball statistician Bill James. He wanted to know how much a player contributed to the main purpose of a baseball team's offense: scoring runs. Hockey's Goals Created metric attempts to accomplish the same thing by determining how a player contributes to a team's offense by helping the team score goals. Much like Runs Created, which has seen many iterations and improvements since its creation, there is no right way to calculate Goals Created. Alan Ryder has used two different methods. The first involves attributing a percentage of each goal to the second assist, the first assist and the goal itself, while adjusting for situational factors such as whether or not a team is short-handed or on the power play. Ryder's second method is represented by the formula:

Goals Created = 0.5 * (Player Goals + Player Assists/ (Team Assists/Team Goals))

A player's Goals Created (GC) is calculated separately by situation, then summed:

Total GC = GC even strength + GC on the power play + GC short-handed

The only problem with Ryder's different versions of Goals Created is their relative complexity. They're not exactly something the average person could calculate on a napkin. And breaking the statistic down by situation may be a boon to precision, but it requires a bit more work. So instead, we'll use the Goals Created formula created by the folks at Hockey-Reference.com. This version also deals with the problem of the relative weighting of goals and assists. More importantly, the Goals

Created data is readily available from their web-site, no calculations necessary. Here is the formula:

Goals Created = (Goals + (Assists * 0.5)) * (Team Goals/ (Team Goals + (Team Assists * 0.5)))

You might notice that the formula attributes one "point" for a goal and half a "point" for an assist in the calculation. Yet the formula is more nuanced than that. Let's look at some examples to see how Goals Created deals with a player's offense, starting with two fictional teammates, Kurtis and Scott:

Table 11						
	GP	G	A	P	Team Goals	Team Assists
Kurtis	82	40	40	80	200	300
Scott	82	20	60	80	200	300

Since Kurtis and Scott play for the same team, team goals and team assists are the same for both players. They also played in the exact same number of games, as well as scored the same number of points—as points are traditionally calculated. The difference is that Kurtis scored more goals, while Scott got more assists. When we run the data through the Goals Created formula, we get:

Table 12	
	GC
Kurtis	34.29
Scott	28.57

Something to note is the decrease in the magnitude of Goals Created relative to the players' conventional point totals. Both Kurtis and Scott scored 80 points each, yet their Goals Created totals are below 35. This is a result of how Goals Created deals with a goal. Instead of each goal or assist being worth one "point," Goals Created credits each team goal scored as one unit, then divides that single team-goal unit among the players involved. For example, if Kurtis scores a goal and Scott gets the only assist, Kurtis gets credit for 0.66 Goals Created and Scott gets the rest, 0.33 Goals Created. Their team total is one Goal Created. One goal scored, one Goal Created. It makes a lot of sense.

On an individual level, the results of the calculation tell us that Kurtis was more valuable than Scott in terms of our metric. Kurtis is 17 percent more valuable, in fact. If you think about it, this is a very satisfying result. Analyzing the players by goals alone tells us that Kurtis is twice as productive as Scott. If total points is the metric observed, Kurtis and Scott are equally valuable. Intuition says that their relative worth should be somewhere in between these results. Goals Created gives us that outcome. It says that Kurtis' 80 points, conventionally calculated, are more beneficial to the team than Scott's.

Now you have a better measure of offensive ability to help you determine who was the best performing forward last season (2006–07, for our purposes) and who is the best free-agent forward to fill a spot on your roster. Here are the UFAs, sorted by Goals Created:

Table 13				
Player	G	A	P	GC
Joe Sakic	36	64	100	36.08
Daniel Briere	32	63	95	33.21
Pavel Datsyuk	27	60	87	30.81
Ray Whitney	32	51	83	30.78
Michael Nylander	26	57	83	29.23
Vyacheslav Kozlov	28	52	80	29.16
Jason Blake	40	29	69	28.70
Chris Drury	37	32	69	27.72
Ryan Smyth	36	32	68	27.69
Paul Kariya	24	52	76	26.24
Bill Guerin	36	20	56	24.64
Brendan Shanahan	29	33	62	24.12
Keith Tkachuk	27	31	58	22.91
Dainius Zubrus	24	36	60	22.91
Viktor Kozlov	25	26	51	20.25
Petr Sykora	22	31	53	19.68
Scott Gomez	13	47	60	18.72
Ladislav Nagy	12	43	55	17.60
Mike Comrie	20	25	45	17.55
Jeff O'Neill	20	22	42	16.28
Scott Hartnell	22	17	39	16.00

Table 13 cont.			
Player	G	A	P	GC
Mike Johnson	11	20	31	11.20
Michael Peca	4	11	15	4.90
Todd Bertuzzi	3	8	11	3.75
Michal Handzus	3	5	8	3.04

Once again, we can use rates to organize the free-agent forwards by their efficiency in Goals Created by taking ice time into account to get Goals Created per 60 minutes:

Table 14			
Player	G	A	P	GC/60
Joe Sakic	36	64	100	1.308
Daniel Briere	32	63	95	1.274
Ray Whitney	32	51	83	1.219
Pavel Datsyuk	27	60	87	1.172
Jason Blake	40	29	69	1.157
Chris Drury	37	32	69	1.150
Bill Guerin	36	20	56	1.129
Ryan Smyth	36	32	68	1.129
Brendan Shanahan	29	33	62	1.090
Michael Nylander	26	57	83	1.089
Michal Handzus	3	5	8	1.086
Mike Comrie	20	25	45	1.063
Vyacheslav Kozlov	28	52	80	1.054
Keith Tkachuk	27	31	58	0.995
Jeff O'Neill	20	22	42	0.961

| Table 14 cont. | | | |
Player	G	A	P	GC/60
Scott Hartnell	22	17	39	0.954
Paul Kariya	24	52	76	0.942
Todd Bertuzzi	3	8	11	0.938
Viktor Kozlov	25	26	51	0.914
Dainius Zubrus	24	36	60	0.893
Petr Sykora	22	31	53	0.864
Scott Gomez	13	47	60	0.824
Ladislav Nagy	12	43	55	0.762
Mike Johnson	11	20	31	0.546
Michael Peca	4	11	15	0.483

Thirty-seven-year-old Sakic refuses to be shaken from the top of the free-agent list. Managing to pop into the top five, from 10th place on the points-per-60-minutes list (Table 10), is Blake.

Thus far we've managed to fool around with players' first-order statistics in an attempt to remove some of the bias inherent in those stats. The usage of rates tries to level the playing field between first-, second-, third- and fourth-liners. The Goals Created formula assigns an appropriate value to an assist, giving us a more accurate representation of a player's offensive contribution. Both strategies will help you in your quest to compare forwards when attempting to plug the hole in your roster—but we can still do better.

WHY BOTHER WITH HOCKEYNOMICS?   67

All Minutes Are NOT Created Equal

An air of anticipation envelopes the arena as the players line up for a center-ice faceoff. Dave Bolland has just given the Chicago Blackhawks a 3–2 lead over the Vancouver Canucks in a crucial game six. With five minutes remaining on the clock, there's plenty of time for Vancouver to score a goal, but not enough for them to avoid feeling the burden of pressure. The puck drops, plays around in the neutral ice area and eventually makes its way deep into the Blackhawks' zone. Canucks center Ryan Kesler, in hot pursuit, catches up with the Chicago defender behind the net and attempts a check. The whistle blows, and the referee signals a holding call on Kesler. The arena erupts in jeers. Kesler's linemate, Alex Burrows, smashes his stick against the glass in a fit of rage. The Vancouver fans go berserk, littering the ice with debris, causing a five-minute delay of the game, all in reaction to the penalty. What's the big deal?

The problem doesn't need a whole lot of explanation. The Canucks needed a goal, and time was limited. Incurring a penalty at that point in the game made scoring that goal far more difficult. As it turned out in reality, the Canucks killed the penalty but ran out of time, losing game six to the 'Hawks 4–2. The Vancouver players and fans reacted because they understood how a penalty changes the dynamic of play.

A hockey game can be broken down into three different sub-games, or situations. Most of the game is played five on five, or even strength. In this scenario, there is a strategic balance between scoring and preventing goals. But a not-insignificant proportion of a hockey game is played when one team or the other receives a penalty. The team that incurs that penalty must play some amount of time short-handed, while the other team gains a man advantage. The goals of a team in one of these three situations—even strength, short-handed, power play—are different. On the power play, the team with the man advantage tries to score. Because that team has an extra player, scoring is easier and defense is less important. The other side of that coin is playing short-handed. Offense is less pressing, and the goal is to survive the penalty without the other team scoring.

Because the dynamics of the game change so much when a penalty is called, we should take it into consideration when analyzing players. First, scoring is easier with an extra player, and much more difficult when killing a penalty. This has to affect a player's statistics, depending on how his ice time is allocated among the three situations I described. Second, a player can't directly control his ice time, or more importantly, his special-teams ice time. Those decisions are made by the coaching staff.

What I'm trying to explain, long-windedly, is that all minutes of ice time are not the same. That might be a problem, because we use ice time in our Goals Created per 60 minutes calculation, which is, up to this point, the metric helping you decide which player to sign. We expect a player to score more in proportion to how much power-play ice time he gets. We also expect a player to score less if he spends a lot of his time on the ice killing penalties. Therefore, we should consider this aspect when trying to establish which free-agent forward will produce the most value.

So how much easier is it to score on a power play? Five times? Fifty times? Ask 10 different hockey fans, and you're likely to get 10 different answers. The same idea applies when considering the increase in difficulty in scoring while on the penalty kill. To get a more objective answer, we should do what analysts do and dig into the data. One method is to add up all the even-strength time on ice over a particular time span, as well as the even-strength goals over the same period. From there, the average even-strength goal-scoring rate can be determined by dividing the goals by time on ice. Next, we need to do the same calculation for the other two situations—short-handed and power play. Once the goal-scoring rates from each situation are calculated, we can figure out the relative difficulty of scoring in each situation by the ratios of the goal-scoring rates. For example, if power plays result in 10 goals per minute, and even-strength play results in two goals per minute, we can say that it's five times easier to score on a power play than it is to score at even strength.

It turns out that when this analysis is done over a period between 2000 and 2006, there are about 2.5 more goals per minute on the power play than at even strength. Meanwhile, there are only about 0.4 goals scored short-handed for every one goal scored at even strength per minute of situational ice time. Just as expected, it's much easier to score on the power play and much harder to score while killing a penalty.

Now we need to apply what we've determined about ice time into our analysis of the free-agent forwards. I hope I have convinced you that Goals Created per 60 minutes is a decent measure of a player's offensive abilities. But now we've discovered this little issue with the type of minutes a player plays. If a player gets a lot of power-play time, we expect more Goals Created output, right? Well, the way our Goals Created per

60 minutes metric works is by rewarding players who play relatively less ice time. Let's look at Kurtis and Scott in a new scenario.

Table 15			
	GC	TOI	GC/60
Kurtis	30	1000	1.8
Scott	35	1500	1.4

Kurtis has fewer Goals Created than Scott, but he has also created those goals in a shorter amount of ice time. Therefore, the metric says Kurtis is more valuable, represented by his higher GC/60. Now, let's apply what we've determined about situational ice time:

Table 16					
	GC	ES TOI	PP TOI	TOI	GC/60
Kurtis	30	1000	0	1000	1.8
Scott	30	500	500	1000	1.8

Here Kurtis and Scott have the same number of Goals Created, the same number of minutes on the ice and hence the same number of Goals Created per 60 minutes. But Scott played half his time on the ice on the power play. We know it's easier to score on the power play, so shouldn't that be represented in Scott's Goals Created? It should, but our metric tells us that these players are equally valuable. How can we fix this?

Since we know that scoring is 2.5 times easier on the power play, we can assume that one minute on the power play will produce as many goals as two-and-a-half minutes at even strength. Therefore, we can adjust Scott's power-play minutes by multiplying them by 2.5. This has the effect of "normalizing" his power-play minutes. In essence, it punishes a player for every minute he's on the power play. We know it's easier to score, so if that player isn't scoring more often, there's a problem. Here's Kurtis and Scott after the adjustment:

Table 17					
	GC	ES TOI	PP TOI	ADJ TOI	GC/60
Kurtis	30	1000	0	1000	1.8
Scott	30	500	500	1750	1.0

ADJ TOI stands for "Adjusted Time on Ice" and is calculated here as:

$$\text{ADJ TOI} = \text{Even Strength Time on Ice} + (\text{Power Play Time on Ice} * 2.5)$$

Scott's 500 minutes on the power play are equivalent to 1250 minutes of even-strength time. This cranks up his total time on ice and, as such, his GC/60 suffers. The results agree with what we've assumed. Kurtis is more valuable than Scott because he is able to create as many goals as Scott while playing all his time at even strength, whereas Scott plays half his time in offensively favorable situations.

To adjust for penalty killing, we can do the same thing. A player's offensive measures shouldn't suffer because he spends a lot of his ice time killing penalties. Penalty killing is an important aspect of hockey, but the goal isn't to generate offense. A penalty-killing success is measured by defense; if the other team doesn't score, you are successful. So to adjust for penalty-killing minutes, knowing that it's much harder to score while short-handed, we use the formula:

ADJ TOI = Even Strength Time on Ice + (Power Play Time on Ice * 2.5) + (Short-handed Time on Ice * 0.4)

The 0.4 coefficient is our measure of the relative difficulty of scoring on the penalty kill, explained above. Whereas multiplying power-play minutes by 2.5 inflates ADJ TOI, thus lowering GC/60, the short-handed adjustment decreases ADJ TOI. All else being equal, this results in a higher Goals Created per 60 minutes value. Players are rewarded offensively for spending lots of time killing penalties. For good measure, we'll take another look at our fictional players:

Table 18						
	GC	ES TOI	PP TOI	SH TOI	ADJ TOI	ADJ GC/60
Kurtis	50	1000	0	750	1300	2.3
Scott	50	500	1000	250	3100	1.0

Each player created 50 goals, and each player played 1750 minutes. But Kurtis did so while playing most of his time at even strength and the remaining minutes killing penalties. Scott spent more than half of his time on the power play, with a bit at even strength and an even smaller amount on the penalty kill. As such, our Goals Created per 60 minutes metric (GC/60), adjusted for situational ice time (ADJ GC/60), tells us that Kurtis is far more valuable than Scott: 2.3 ADJ GC/60 to 1.0 ADJ GC/60.

Now we need to see how this adjustment affects you and your quest to find a free-agent forward. Your best bet is to get the office whipping boy to gather up the situational ice-time data. It's readily available from the NHL, but getting information is what you pay your gofer for. Once all the data are rounded up and the ice time of our list of the top 25 free agents is adjusted, the result is:

Table 19		
Player	ADJ TOI	ADJ GC/60
Joe Sakic	2252.6	0.961
Pavel Datsyuk	1958.9	0.944
Daniel Briere	2127.1	0.937
Todd Bertuzzi	246.0	0.915
Chris Drury	1820.4	0.914
Ryan Smyth	1863.2	0.892
Jason Blake	1951.2	0.883

Table 19 cont.		
Player	ADJ TOI	ADJ GC/60
Ray Whitney	2118.0	0.872
Bill Guerin	1740.4	0.849
Michal Handzus	216.6	0.842
Brendan Shanahan	1744.7	0.829
Mike Comrie	1306.9	0.806
Viktor Kozlov	1518.1	0.800
Vyacheslav Kozlov	2211.4	0.791
Michael Nylander	2253.8	0.778
Scott Hartnell	1281.1	0.749
Keith Tkachuk	1839.8	0.747
Jeff O'Neill	1346.9	0.725
Paul Kariya	2266.5	0.695
Dainius Zubrus	2060.2	0.667
Petr Sykora	1930.3	0.612
Scott Gomez	1844.2	0.609
Ladislav Nagy	1819.8	0.580
Mike Johnson	1168.9	0.575
Michael Peca	540.0	0.544

Who the heck is this Sakic fellow? Whoever he is, he's pretty good. He's managed to top the list since we included total points in our analysis, and with the list organized by ADJ GC/60 (Adjusted Goals Created per 60 minutes), he maintains his toehold at the top. An interesting surprise is the surge of Todd Bertuzzi. Recall that when we looked at our players by goal-scoring rate, Bertuzzi was at the bottom of the list. Now that we've taken assists into account through Goals Created, as well as adjusted ice time according to situation, Bertuzzi reveals his offensive value, despite having played few games. That's something to think about as you ponder which free agent best fits into the lineup.

By now you might have noticed something odd. As you've watched the players at the top of the list move around with our statistical adjustments, there have been a few constants. Yes, Sakic, Daniel Briere and Pavel Datsyuk are great players and deserve their place. But maintaining their positions at the *bottom*, list after list, are two players: Mike Johnson and Michael Peca. It's true that every list has to have someone in the bottom positions, but this isn't just any old list. This is a list of the top 25 free agents from the 2007 off-season. Why are Johnson and Peca on this list? The only answer is that these players have a skill that, up until now, our analysis hasn't been able to account for.

De-fense! De-fense!

Earlier, I explained the importance of scoring goals. It's impossible to win a hockey game without scoring; the best you can do is tie. Therefore, if you're trying to win games, goal scoring, especially when dealing with forwards, is an important measure of value. But there's an obvious flipside to that argument. If a team can only win by outscoring the opposition, then preventing goals will also result in wins. In other words, a team with an average offense and a stellar defense should be as competitive as a team with an average defense and an amazing offense.

The problem is that defense in hockey is extremely difficult to measure. Theory construes that it's important, watching a hockey game reveals that certain players are good at it and awards are presented based on it—yet we can't seem to put a number on it. This allows subjectivity to creep into our judgments. Hockey fans are forced to either ignore defense, or put their faith in convoluted measures of it. Neither option is ideal.

A statistic regularly touted as a measure of defense is a player's plus-minus rating. There are a number of problems with using plus-minus as an indicator of defense, and the main one is that, by definition, half of a player's plus-minus rating is offense. Think about the absurdity of that. Better yet, let's examine it:

Table 20			
	GF	GA	+/-
Kurtis	10	5	5
Scott	180	174	6

Assuming that both players have the same amount of ice time, which player is the better defender? Plus-minus rating tells us that Scott is, but what does your gut say? Mine says Kurtis. Scott was on the ice for nearly 35 times as many goals as Kurtis in the same amount of ice time. How on earth can we say that Scott is better at defense? It makes no sense, but as a measurement of defense, that's what plus-minus tells us.

There are other problems associated with the plus-minus rating as a defensive metric, and among them is that plus-minus is very reliant on the team element, both the player's own and the opposition's. To prevent discrepancies such as those described here, we can choose to ignore defense altogether, which is what we've done thus far in helping you choose the best free-agent forward. But much like ignoring assists in offensive production, ignoring defense when trying to put a value on a player is going to cause some problems, especially for guys like Peca.

Peca's bread and butter has always been in the defensive part of the game, even though his offense was never terrible, especially in his junior years. I have to admit I'm slightly biased, since I've always likened my hockey skill set to Peca's and guys like him: win faceoffs, work hard, hit, score the odd goal. I was also lucky enough to see Peca play for the Sudbury Wolves early in his career. To this day, measuring "hard work" by actually watching hockey is more accurate than any metrics we have. Unfortunately, it's impossible to watch enough hockey to evaluate every player's defensive ability. Some people try, and award trophies like the Selke (which Peca has won twice) on that basis. But this doesn't help us when trying to evaluate Peca relative to players who score a lot more than he does.

In order to level the playing field, we need to create some kind of method to measure defense. Since there aren't any simple measures out there, we'll have to make it up as we go, based on logic and rationale. This isn't as hard as it sounds, and isn't unlike what we've done so far during your imagined tenure as an NHL general manager. For example, we first looked at goals, but logic dictated that goals weren't enough. Bingo!—we used Goals Created. Among our calculations we used a player's time on the ice, but rationale told us that all minutes were not the same. So we introduced adjusted ice-time figures to compensate for playing short-handed or on the power play. We'll do the same here. Besides, by establishing your own system of doing something, you'll set yourself apart from another GM who might not be as clever. That gives you an efficiency advantage.

The first order of business is to establish exactly what we're trying to determine with the defensive metric. If offense is considered the ability to produce goals and we use Goals Created to measure that production, then what we're looking for to measure defense is a sort of backwards Goals Created. The idea is that each player who is on the ice for a goal against has to take partial blame for that goal. Maybe a player didn't backcheck hard enough, maybe he got beat by a nice play, maybe he wasn't covering his point man or maybe he even buried the puck in his own net. Goals Created tells us how one offensive goal is divided up between the players who contributed to it, for example, assigning 0.5 Goals Created to the goal scorer and 0.25 Goals Created to each of the two players who added an assist. Our defensive metric should do the same, by dividing one goal against into a fraction and dispersing it across the players on the ice. The question is, how do we divide up the goal against?

If we had unlimited data, unlimited computing power and unlimited time, the solution would be to look at every goal scored over the period in question—a game, a season, a career—and then break up the individual goals accordingly. Here's an example of how that might work: on one play, a defenseman attempts to wrap the puck behind his own net and ends up scoring on his own unsuspecting goaltender. Okay, so that's easy, this guy gets 1.0 goal against. But wait—should the goalie have been paying closer attention? In case he wasn't, let's give the defenseman 0.9 goals against and the goaltender 0.1 goals against. But now, what about the left-winger, who in an attempt to clear the puck from the zone, poked it to the opposing defender, who dumped it back in the corner, forcing the defenseman to attempt to clear the puck around his net? Maybe we can give the left-winger 0.2 goals against, the goalie 0.1 goals against and the defenseman who scored in his own net 0.7 goals against. Okay, sure, but now what about the centerman who lost the faceoff just seconds before the winger tried to clear that puck...?

You can see the difficulty—nigh, impossibility—of attempting to assign blame in this manner. Something far easier to calculate is the *average* blame per player on the ice at the time of the goal against. Instead of looking at each goal on an individual level, we can look at all the goals scored against a team, and all the players who were on the ice during every one of those goals, and determine, on average, what proportion of a goal against should be attributed to each player. Using the average is not only far easier, but it makes intuitive sense as well. It implies that every goal scored against a player's team while that player was on the ice could have been prevented, at some point, by that player. Another advantage is that although there are certainly times when a player deserves much of the blame for a goal, there are other times when he deserves little. Using the average deals with both of these situations. To calculate the goals against average, we can use the formula:

Goals Against = Player's Goals Against * (Team Goals Against/Total Player's Goals Against)

Some of those terms look similar, so I'll explain. Player's Goals Against is the total number of goals that an individual player was on the ice for over a season. It includes even-strength, power-play and short-handed goals against. Team Goals Against is the total number of goals scored against the team. This is the number you get by adding up the opponent's score from each game. Total Player's Goals Against is the sum of all the individual players' goals against totals for the team, including the goalies. For example, if a team is scored against at even strength, there is only one Team Goals Against, but six (one for each position) Player's Goals Against assigned. Let's look at our fictional teammates:

Table 21				
	PGA	TGA	TPGA	GA
Kurtis	45	250	1200	9.4
Scott	62	250	1200	12.9

Kurtis was on the ice for 45 goals and Scott was on the ice for 62. Our Goals Against formula tells us that Kurtis was personally responsible for 9.4 goals, Scott 12.9. The calculation is similar to that of Goals Created, but for goal prevention.

The Goals Against formula is not without its flaws. One problem is that it assumes each position is equally responsible for defense, which is usually not the case in reality. Common sense tells us that a defenseman should shoulder more of the defensive burden than a forward. A goalie should bear the most responsibility, since his sole objective is goal prevention. These issues will cause some problems if we try to compare the metric across positions, but since we're dealing only with forwards, they shouldn't be fatal.

Another separate problem is the difficulty of calculation. Like Goals Created, the Goals Against formula is a bit complicated, and since the data is not out there, waiting to be culled from the Internet, the formula is being created, here, on the fly. It turns out, however, that this new measure, "Kinda Goals Created Against" (KGCA), can be reasonably estimated by dividing Player's Goals Against by six. I took the liberty of examining a sample of 50 NHL teams between 1990–91 and 2007–08. The average portion of a goal against assigned to an individual over the sample was 0.179. Across the 50 teams, that number never fluctuated outside 0.172 and 0.188. Dividing a player's goals against by six implies an average attribution of 0.167, which is pretty close to the actual values. It also makes the calculation far simpler.

We now have a method of assigning personal blame to goals scored against a team. Here's the list of the top 25 free-agent forwards again, along with their "Kinda Goals Created Against," which is calculated by dividing each Player's Goals Against by six:

Table 22

Player	KGCA	Player	KGCA
Michal Handzus	1.17	Ladislav Nagy	9.00
Todd Bertuzzi	1.50	Brendan Shanahan	9.17
Scott Hartnell	4.83	Petr Sykora	9.67
Bill Guerin	6.50	Jason Blake	10.00
Michael Peca	6.67	Paul Kariya	10.17
Jeff O'Neill	6.67	Vyacheslav Kozlov	10.67
Mike Comrie	6.83	Ryan Smyth	10.83
Keith Tkachuk	6.83	Daniel Briere	10.83
Scott Gomez	7.50	Ray Whitney	11.83
Mike Johnson	8.00	Joe Sakic	13.00
Pavel Datsyuk	8.17	Chris Drury	13.17
Michael Nylander	8.50	Dainius Zubrus	13.83
Viktor Kozlov	8.67		

A clever reader will note that simply taking a player's goals against and dividing it by six is a ridiculous method of measuring defensive value. And that reader is right. This is clear from the list, which places those with the fewest minutes played—recall Handzus and Bertuzzi played fewer games because of injuries—at the top. By now it should be clear that we have to make an adjustment for ice time (rates matter!). We've also established that, since all ice time isn't the same, we need to adjust the individual minutes played based on situations. These adjustments will make our metric more useful.

Instinct might tell you that we've already done this work, that the minutes played have already been adjusted situationally. However, recall what we did when we adapted those minutes played. At that time, we were dealing with offense. As such, our adjustment involved punishing players who played a lot of power-play minutes and rewarding players who played a lot of short-handed minutes. We did so because we expected players to produce more offense on the power play than on the penalty kill. Therefore, we multiplied power-play minutes by 2.5 and short-handed minutes by 0.4. This time, though, we're looking at goal prevention, or Kinda Goals Created Against in particular. But unlike Goals Created, it is preferable to have a relatively low Kinda Goals Created Against value.

So while we still need to reward defenders who play a lot of penalty-killing minutes—it's more difficult to defend goals when short-handed—and punish those who give up goals while on the man advantage, we need to flip-flop the ice-time adjustment. Instead of multiplying power-play minutes by 2.5, we will divide them by 2.5. This means that a player who goes one minute on the power play without a goal against doesn't get as much credit as a player who goes one minute at even strength without having a goal scored against him. The same procedure is done for penalty-killing minutes, dividing them by 0.4 rather than multiplying. Here's Kurtis and Scott to clarify:

Table 23					
	PGA	PP TOI	SH TOI	ES TOI	TOI
Kurtis	15	0	50	100	150
Scott	15	100	0	50	150

Both Kurtis and Scott are personally to blame for 15 goals each. Kurtis has given up those 15 goals while playing one-third of his ice time killing penalties, the rest at even strength. His teammate Scott is personally responsible for the exact same number of goals, but Scott has spent most of his ice time on the power play and none killing penalties. Who is the better defender? Clearly it's Kurtis, who is blamed for the same number of goals as Scott, but in situations more conducive to his opponents scoring. Look what happens when we use our old ADJ TOI value:

Table 24						
	PGA	PP TOI	SH TOI	ES TOI	ADJ TOI	KGCA
Kurtis	15	0	50	100	120	7.50
Scott	15	100	0	50	300	3.00

When we adjust the players' ice time in the manner we used for the offense-based ADJ GC/60, KGCA tells us that Scott has a better rating than Kurtis. Yet we know that Kurtis defends in tougher situations than Scott, and thus deserves more credit. When we recalculate the data by dividing by the situational coefficients (2.5 for the power play, 0.4 for the penalty kill), the players look different:

Table 25						
	PGA	PP TOI	SH TOI	ES TOI	ADJ TOI	KGCA/60
Kurtis	15	0	50	100	225	4.00
Scott	15	100	0	50	90	10.00

That's more like it. With that slight change, our metric makes more sense. KGCA now says that Kurtis will be on the ice for, on average, 4 goals per 60 minutes, regardless of the situation. Scott will be on the ice for 10. Either Scott is a relatively poor defender or very unlucky. In either case, it's probably best to have Kurtis on the ice in a situation where goal prevention is important.

Now that we've made the pertinent alterations to our ice-time calculation, we can determine the KGCA rates for our 25 free agents:

Table 26

Player	KGCA/60	Player	KGCA/60
Scott Hartnell	0.286	Ryan Smyth	0.426
Pavel Datsyuk	0.302	Ladislav Nagy	0.428
Mike Johnson	0.313	Jason Blake	0.450
Keith Tkachuk	0.338	Jeff O'Neill	0.452
Bill Guerin	0.339	Mike Comrie	0.459
Viktor Kozlov	0.370	Daniel Briere	0.474
Michael Nylander	0.375	Michael Peca	0.479
Todd Bertuzzi	0.379	Chris Drury	0.495
Scott Gomez	0.383	Petr Sykora	0.505
Michal Handzus	0.388	Joe Sakic	0.527
Brendan Shanahan	0.397	Ray Whitney	0.549
Vyacheslav Kozlov	0.400	Dainius Zubrus	0.598
Paul Kariya	0.414		

Quite a few movers and shakers on this list! Finally, Peca climbs his way out of the cellar, jumping up a few positions. It turns out that Sakic gives up a lot of goals per 60 minutes despite his dominant offense—he has the third highest KGCA/60 on the list. Johnson, another player known for his defensive abilities, gets some credit at the top and appears in third place. Hartnell—who was already mentioned for his scoring efficiency—and Selke-winner Datsyuk round out the top three.

Now we need to figure out how to roll KGCA/60 into the analysis in order to help fill in your roster. By itself, the metric is slightly lacking in that we don't really know what a "good" value is. We know that Tkachuk, relative to Scott Gomez, gives up fewer goals per 60 minutes. But is Tkachuk's 0.338 KGCA/60 enough for us to consider him a good defender, or is he just one of the best of a group of lousy players?

Remember what it takes to win hockey games. First and foremost, you need to score goals. This is offense, and we've chosen to measure it through ADJ GC/60, or Goals Created per 60 minutes, adjusted by situation. Second, you need to prevent goals. This is defense, and we're measuring it through KGCA/60, or Kinda Goals Created Against per 60 minutes. On a team level, all that is necessary to win a game is to outscore the opponent. Therefore, a player's purpose is to put up more offense than he allows the opposing players to contribute (which is, really, just another way of saying defense). Because some players, like the goaltender, are confined to this one aspect of the game, defense, the rest of the players have to make up for it with more offense. You want players who produce a lot of offense while preventing as much scoring as possible from the other team; you want high ADJ GC/60 and low KGCA/60.

By subtracting KGCA/60 from ADJ GC/60 we can see which players produce more offense than they allow and by how much. The number obtained is equal to a player's Net Goals per 60 minutes. If this value is positive, then a player is contributing positively to the team. The nice thing about this metric is that a player can increase his Net Goals per 60 minutes by either getting more points or by preventing more goals. This is exactly what we want to see, since accomplishing either is beneficial to the team.

Here's the list of free agents, listed with their ADJ GC/60, KGCA/60 and the difference between the two:

Table 27

Player	ADJ GC/60	KGCA/60	Net G/60
Pavel Datsyuk	0.944	0.302	0.642
Todd Bertuzzi	0.915	0.379	0.536
Bill Guerin	0.849	0.339	0.511
Ryan Smyth	0.892	0.426	0.465
Scott Hartnell	0.749	0.286	0.463
Daniel Briere	0.937	0.474	0.463
Michal Handzus	0.842	0.388	0.454
Joe Sakic	0.961	0.527	0.434
Jason Blake	0.883	0.450	0.432

Table 27 cont.			
Player	ADJ GC/60	KGCA/60	Net G/60
Brendan Shanahan	0.829	0.397	0.432
Viktor Kozlov	0.800	0.370	0.430
Chris Drury	0.914	0.495	0.418
Keith Tkachuk	0.747	0.338	0.410
Michael Nylander	0.778	0.375	0.404
Vyacheslav Kozlov	0.791	0.400	0.391
Mike Comrie	0.806	0.459	0.346
Ray Whitney	0.872	0.549	0.323
Paul Kariya	0.695	0.414	0.280
Jeff O'Neill	0.725	0.452	0.273
Mike Johnson	0.575	0.313	0.262
Scott Gomez	0.609	0.383	0.226
Ladislav Nagy	0.580	0.428	0.152
Petr Sykora	0.612	0.505	0.107
Dainius Zubrus	0.667	0.598	0.070
Michael Peca	0.544	0.479	0.066

Let's look at an example from the list to explain what we have here. By taking Comrie's 20 goals and 25 assists and converting them into Goals Created, then taking those Goals Created and adjusting for ice time, we obtained a ADJ GC/60 of 0.806. That's Comrie's offense. Then, we took all the goals against that he was on the ice for and turned those into KGCA. We adjusted *this* value for situational ice time and obtained a KGCA/60 of 0.459. That's the offense of his opponents, or his defense. When we subtract Comrie's KGCA/60 from his ADJ GC/60, we get 0.346. For every 60 minutes of ice time that Comrie gets, he contributes slightly more than one-third of a goal created after his opponent's offense is considered. That's his Net Goals per 60 minutes (Net G/60).

So much for my icon, Peca, though. He did contribute positively to his team, producing 0.066 Net G/60, but he's still holding down the bottom of the list. I guess we'll have to chalk it up to a rough season.

Detroit Red Wings centerman Datsyuk displays his mettle in both aspects of the hockey game. Thanks to his extremely high ADJ GC/60 and low KGCA/60, our metric tells us that Datsyuk produces about 0.6 Net G/60. Lagging behind him is Bertuzzi, whose ice time was limited but who still managed to produce in the games he played. Guerin and Smyth both have strong showings, as does Hartnell on the strength of the lowest KGCA/60 on the list. Offensive powerhouses Drury and Sakic slipped a few spots because of their lack of defense.

At the outset of this little experiment—putting you in the driver's seat of an NHL front office—we defined our purpose as finding the best forward for your money. The problem was with how to define the "best." Clearly, offense was important, so we set about finding a good measure of offensive contribution on an individual level. We looked at goals, points, scoring rates and, eventually, Goals Created. But scoring 100 goals while allowing 150 won't win you many games, and thus we searched for a metric that portrayed a forward's ability to prevent goals. That journey ended with Kinda Goals Created Against. By calculating the difference between the two metrics ADJ GC/60 and KGCA/60 we are now able to see which players are best at helping you with your assignment—win games. Yet I get the feeling that something is still missing...

Show Me the Money!

Right. Your boss tasked you with finding the best forward *for the money*. Net G/60 might tell you which players are the best, but it doesn't take into account how much that quality is going to cost. And in a budget-constrained world, cost is crucial. Teams have a limit on the amount of money they are able to spend on players, and it's called the salary cap. It's all well and good to figure out who the best player is, and it's normal to want to sign him, but the most important consideration is whether or not your team can afford him. As set out in the rules of this thought experiment, the team owner has authorized the use of a little over $6 million in cap space. One of the advantages of traveling back in time to the 2007 off-season for this assignment is that we are able to see the value of the contracts the free-agent list actually signed. Assuming you have to beat the players' actual contract offer by five percent, here are the "predicted" salaries of the 25 free agents:

Table 28			
Player	**Offer**	**Player**	**Offer**
Daniel Briere	$8,190,000	Todd Bertuzzi	$4,200,000
Scott Gomez	$7,728,000	Michal Handzus	$4,200,000
Chris Drury	$7,402,500	Ladislav Nagy	$3,937,500
Pavel Datsyuk	$7,035,000	Vyacheslav Kozlov	$3,843,000
Ryan Smyth	$6,562,500	Ray Whitney	$3,727,500
Joe Sakic	$6,300,000	Dainius Zubrus	$3,570,000
Paul Kariya	$6,300,000	Mike Comrie	$3,543,750
Scott Hartnell	$5,145,000	Brendan Shanahan	$2,625,000
Michael Nylander	$5,118,750	Viktor Kozlov	$2,625,000
Bill Guerin	$4,725,000	Petr Sykora	$2,625,000
Jason Blake	$4,200,000	Michael Peca	$2,100,000
Keith Tkachuk	$4,200,000	Mike Johnson	$787,500
Jeff O'Neill	$4,200,000		

The range of prices that these guys are worth should immediately jump out at you. It should also be obvious that a few are completely out of your budget. For instance, Net G/60 leader Datsyuk is asking for more than $7 million. You also predict that you'll need to offer Briere about $8 million a season to get him to sign a contract with your team, an amount that is well beyond your means. At the other end of the spectrum is Johnson, who you can get for a song. Which player is worth your money?

That question is the most vital component of this entire exercise. How much value will be gained from the employment of each of these players? To figure this out, let's transform the players' Net G/60 minutes into something more manageable. We can do so by multiplying this value by 82—the number of games in an NHL season. This gives us the total number of Goals Created, less the total number of Kinda Goals Created Against, with the player on the ice for 60 minutes of every game over a full 82-game schedule. There are two advantages to doing this: it normalizes the data as well as eliminates a decimal or two. Nobody likes staring at a bunch of decimals.

In order to determine a dollar figure, we can divide the Net Goals over 82 games value by the players' "predicted" salary. Again, to eliminate small decimals, we can multiply the resultant figure by 1,000,000. All this transformation sounds atrocious, but the end result is almost elegant. The value we achieve is equal to the number of Net Goals Created (Net GC) a player will produce, over a full 82-game season, per $1 million in salary. Here's what our list looks like:

Table 29

Player	Net GC/$1 MM	Player	Net GC/$1 MM
Mike Johnson	27.31	Michael Nylander	6.47
Brendan Shanahan	13.50	Ryan Smyth	5.82
Viktor Kozlov	13.45	Joe Sakic	5.65
Todd Bertuzzi	10.46	Jeff O'Neill	5.33
Michal Handzus	8.86	Chris Drury	4.64
Bill Guerin	8.86	Daniel Briere	4.63
Jason Blake	8.44	Paul Kariya	3.65
Vyacheslav Kozlov	8.34	Petr Sykora	3.35
Mike Comrie	8.01	Ladislav Nagy	3.17
Keith Tkachuk	8.00	Michael Peca	2.56
Pavel Datsyuk	7.48	Scott Gomez	2.40
Scott Hartnell	7.38	Dainius Zubrus	1.60
Ray Whitney	7.11		

And there it is: the list that accounts for offense, defense, situational ice time and salary. This list looks quite different from what we started with: simple goals. Most surprising is Johnson. He gets a ton of credit here because he contributes positively with a bit of offense and some good defense, but most importantly of all, he is dirt cheap. As such, it's no contest who you should sign according to our metric: Johnson produces more than twice the value of the next best player, per dollar of salary.

Seasoned veterans Guerin and Brendan Shanahan also seem to turn out good value for the money. Bertuzzi and Handzus, two players who played few games in the 2006–07 data we used for analysis, seem to be good deals if they can shake off their injuries. Datsyuk, the best player in terms of Net Goals Created per 60 minutes, slips down the list a bit because of his high salary, and our offensive powerhouse, Sakic, ends up in 16th place, punished by his big paycheck and seeming lack of ability to prevent goals. Also curious is that the three biggest contracts signed during the 2007 off-season—Briere, Drury and Gomez—offer some of the least value for the money. And, of course, I'm happy to say that Peca doesn't come in dead last.

So, you've done all the research and have an answer for your boss—it's time to take your work in and show him your magnificent findings.

The Magic Formula

You burst into the owner's office, excited for both the outlook of next year's team, as well as your hefty incoming bonus. You explain to your boss that a contract offer should be extended to Johnson first, and if that fails, Shanahan, Viktor Kozlov or Bertuzzi. Your team's owner smiles wryly, reaches into his desk drawer, produces a humidor and offers you a cigar. As you lean back in a fine leather chair, puffing on the expensive cigar, he asks: how did you do it? Your boss wants to know the magic formula.

The reality is that the formula doesn't exist. I certainly wouldn't claim that the little analysis we've done here will prepare you for an NHL front-office position. Hockey, and sports in general, are complicated, and putting numbers on all the factors that contribute to winning is extremely difficult. The statistical analysis of hockey is still in its infancy; stats such as ice time have only been tracked for the last 10 years. If the scale of things we need to know to predetermine a hockey matchup runs from one to 100, we're probably at about five.

With the benefit of hindsight, we can see just how difficult quantifying a player is. The hero of our thought experiment, Johnson, was actually a disaster of a contract. Johnson signed with the St. Louis Blues during the 2007 off-season. He played only 21 games before hurting his shoulder and hasn't played since. At the time of his injury, Johnson had accumulated fewer than two Goals Created. Bad luck, but also demonstrative of how difficult it is to make predictions about the game.

To Err Is Human

Focusing on quantitative methods, we worked so hard to figure out who was the best free-agent forward to sign. That effort led us to a player who dramatically underperformed his projection. What went wrong?

The first problem lies in the bias of our sample. The metrics we developed were intended to find the best free agent available. However, we only applied the metrics to a predetermined list of 25 players. These players were subjectively called "the best." But were they really? Perhaps there were other NHL players who would have performed much better in our metrics than any of the players in the 25-man list. In order to actually figure that out, we'd have to look at all the players in the entire league. That would take tons of time and many, many pages of tables. For our purposes, using a small list of players simplified the process. Still, trying to objectively determine the best player from a subjectively selected shortlist is self-defeating.

Another issue that we have is with explanatory versus predictive measurements. What our analysis has shown is how the top 25 free agents performed in the year studied. It's natural to take this performance and extrapolate it into a prediction, to assume that a player's past results are indicative of his future performance. But this isn't always the case. A common statistic that's often misinterpreted this way is shooting percentage.

On the surface, shooting percentage is an appealing statistic. It's the proportion of shots that a player converts into goals. We tend to believe that good goal scorers must also be accurate shooters. Stop and envision the all-star game's accuracy shootout. This guy hit four targets in five shots, he's good; that guy hit two targets in eight shots, he isn't. But shooting within a hockey game is far less simple than standing in the slot and firing at a stationary target. There is some luck and subjectivity involved (shots are determined by human scorekeepers, after all), and thus there are often big swings in a player's shooting percentage from year to year. Here's the career shooting percentage data from a couple of great goal scorers. The first table represents Brett Hull, the second Wayne Gretzky:

Table 30A: Brett Hull			
Season	G	SOG	SPCT
1986–87	1	5	20.0%
1987–88	32	211	15.2%
1987–88	26	153	17.0%
1987–88	6	58	10.3%
1988–89	41	305	13.4%
1989–90	72	385	18.7%

Table 30A: Brett Hull cont.			
Season	G	SOG	SPCT
1990–91	86	389	22.1%
1991–92	70	408	17.2%
1992–93	54	390	13.8%
1993–94	57	392	14.5%
1994–95	29	200	14.5%
1995–96	43	327	13.1%
1996–97	42	302	13.9%
1997–98	27	211	12.8%
1998–99	32	192	16.7%
1999–00	24	223	10.8%
2000–01	39	219	17.8%
2001–02	30	247	12.1%
2002–03	37	262	14.1%
2003–04	25	200	12.5%
2005–06	0	8	0.0%

Table 30B: Wayne Gretzky			
Season	G	SOG	SPCT
1978–79	46	270	17.0%
1978–79	3	17	17.6%
1978–79	43	253	17.0%
1979–80	51	284	18.0%
1980–81	55	261	21.1%
1981–82	92	369	24.9%
1982–83	71	348	20.4%
1983–84	87	324	26.9%
1984–85	73	358	20.4%
1985–86	52	350	14.9%
1986–87	62	288	21.5%

Table 30B: Wayne Gretzky cont.			
Season	G	SOG	SPCT
1987–88	40	211	19.0%
1988–89	54	303	17.8%
1989–90	40	236	16.9%
1990–91	41	212	19.3%
1991–92	31	215	14.4%
1992–93	16	141	11.3%
1993–94	38	233	16.3%
1994–95	11	142	7.7%
1995–96	23	195	11.8%
1995–96	15	144	10.4%
1995–96	8	51	15.7%
1996–97	25	286	8.7%
1997–98	23	201	11.4%
1998–99	9	132	6.8%

The first thing you should notice is how hard it is to repeat a good shooting percentage performance. In 1990–91, Hull took 389 shots, scoring 86 goals. In 1992–93, he took one more shot but scored 32 fewer goals. What happened?

Gretzky had some similar issues. In 1984–85, he led the league in shots, firing 358 pucks at opposing goaltenders. In the process, he buried 73 goals. The following season, he managed fewer shots, 350, but still led the league in this category. Yet Gretzky scored only 52 times. The year after that, 1986–87, the Great One finished third in the league with 288 shots. Despite the meager shot total, he scored 62 goals. How do we explain this? Was Gretzky a good goal scorer one year, poor the next, then fantastic the year after that? Of course not. Shooting percentage just isn't a good predictive statistic.

Where shooting percentage may have some value, however, is in its explanatory power. Look back at the previous tables for Hull and Gretzky. Notice that in the years each player scores the most goals, their shooting percentage is also high. Perhaps instead of predicting a player's ability to score goals, shooting percentage explains the variation in the number of goals from year to year. If we presume that shooting percentage is somewhat random because of luck and the infinitely different possibilities that are bound to occur from game to game and from season to season, then it's possible that shooting percentage *explains* how a player obtained the goal total he did. After all, Gretzky was the same player between 1984 and 1987, but his goal and shot totals vary drastically. If the explanatory power of shooting percentage is to be believed, it says that in 1984–85 and 1986–87 Gretzky got the right breaks. In 1985–86, he didn't.

This is a subtle but important distinction. You don't want to stake your career on a measurement that doesn't have any ability to show how a player will perform in the future. It may turn out that our metric, Net G/60 (Table 27), does the job of explaining how a well a player did, not how well a player will do.

But shooting percentage introduces a more fundamental problem with the statistical analysis of hockey: random chance. We saw that even when Gretzky took a similar number of shots, he scored a differing number of goals. This occurred because of the random element involved. That random element may separate a good Gretzky season from a great Gretzky season, but it has much larger repercussions for average players.

Most counting statistic totals (goals, assists, etc.) for players are so low that small, random fluctuations can have major effects. Let's say again that Kurtis and Scott are similar players and have each recently signed six-year contracts with their respective teams. For the first five years of their contracts, Kurtis and Scott take a similar number of shots, scoring a similar number of goals:

Table 31

		Goals Scored				
	Year 1	Year 2	Year 3	Year 4	Year 5	Average
Kurtis	13	18	14	17	14	15.2
Scott	14	19	13	13	16	15

Now, in year six, the final year of each of their contracts, Kurtis and Scott want to have big seasons. Their next contract depends on it. Based on Kurtis' yearly average of 15.2 goals, he has about a 10 percent chance of scoring 20 goals (This probability is based on the Poisson Probability Distribution of goal scoring. It is discussed in detail in "Chapter 6: Gretzky's 92—Best Ever?"). Scott's average number of goals over the five-year stretch is 15. While he, like Kurtis, has some probability of scoring 20 goals in the final year of his contract, Scott also has a 10 percent chance of scoring only 10. So what happens if, by pure chance, Kurtis gets lucky and scores 20, while Scott gets unlucky and pots a mere 10? Well, somewhere, an NHL general manager will determine that Kurtis is awesome and sign him to a relatively large contract. On the other hand, Scott might be seen as a player in decline, and he will get a relatively small contract. The problem is that, statistically, there is little difference between these two players. Random variation, or luck, obscures our view.

You might find it odd that these two players, in strict competition with each other for a new contract, end up in a situation where one player gets lucky and the other does not, resulting in a giant disparity between their goal totals. However, in any NHL season, there are many Kurtises and many Scotts, and when you get them all stirring around in the NHL pot, random chance dictates that some of them are going to get 20 goals, and some of them are going to get 10, even if they are equally skilled. So, clearly the 20-goal scorers are not twice as valuable as the 10-goal scorers. It's vital to keep chance in mind when comparing players.

However, there are further issues than the consideration of lucky seasons and plays. There are problems with the actual data in hockey itself. The NHL is only now starting to track some of the important statistics such as ice time and puck possession. The league has recently made public Real Time Scoring Statistics such as hits, give- and take-aways and faceoffs. The relative young age of these stats makes it difficult to use them to draw conclusions because they cover but a small sample of seasons. Only time will solve this problem.

There are also issues within the statistics themselves. What is a hit? What is a take-away? These seem like questions with obvious answers, but there are no hard-and-fast rules; hits, take-aways, etc. are determined subjectively by scorekeepers. Why is a shot taken from outside the offensive zone treated the same as a breakaway shot from point blank? If we're going to put values on players, it has to be easier to differentiate between such obviously unique events. Some of these problems are being resolved, but hockey still has a long way to go.

That's a pretty discouraging list of issues that exist in the analysis of hockey data. It seems that there are nothing but roadblocks preventing us from solving easy questions like, "Which player is the best?" If that's the case, if it's a hopeless venture, why bother? Why analyze the statistics of hockey at all?

We Can Do Better

The point of this thought experiment was to introduce you to the mindset of a hockey analyst. Just because there are issues with the collection and analysis of hockey statistics doesn't mean that the analysis shouldn't be done. Sometimes the statistics we have don't tell us enough. A hockey analyst seeks to gain ever more knowledge and insight into the game. There are no illusions that some magical formula is waiting to be discovered that will tell us all we need to know. Instead, the hope is just to move incrementally up the scale of hockey understanding. If we're at a five on that scale right now, even getting to a six or seven is a great improvement.

The biggest misconception about Michael Lewis' book *Moneyball* was the idea that the Oakland A's'

Billy Beane had uncovered a secret when he and his crew began to emphasize the use of on-base percentage (OBP) in rating players. There was nothing special about OBP. It was a statistic that has been recorded and available for years. What Beane discovered was that OBP was undervalued. This allowed his team to gain an advantage over other teams that didn't value the statistic appropriately. Lewis' story was about exploiting inefficiencies.

And this is why we should analyze hockey: to discover inefficiencies and determine best practices. Hockey is a sport, and sports are all about winning. To win, you need the best players, and finding the best players, as we've seen, isn't easy. The fact of the matter is that NHL teams aren't very good at it, either.

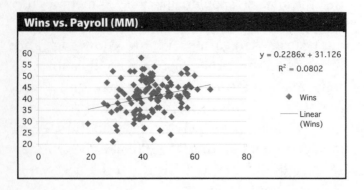

This graph plots all the NHL teams by payroll and the number of games won for every season after the NHL lockout of 2004. If NHL management knew which variables won hockey games, we could assume that a strong relationship existed between wins and payroll; that is, the teams with the highest payrolls would consistently win the most games, and the teams with the lowest payrolls would win the fewest. It turns out that this relationship is extremely weak. If we examine the graph it's clear that payroll and win totals are all over the place.

Sometimes we assume that people in positions of authority automatically know what's best, that all their decisions are sound. This is a fallacy. The evidence tells us that teams don't always spend money on what it takes to win games. Their ineffective ways leave room for the analysts to figure out how to increase efficiency. There is much money to be made and fan loyalty to be earned if a team can get a leg up on the competition, discovering what it truly takes to win. So although our analysis of the 2007 free-agent forwards isn't perfect and told us players like Johnson and Hartnell represent good value—as opposed to players like Gomez and Dainius Zubrus—it is still eons ahead of looking at a simple statistic like goals. And, as I've stressed, getting incrementally better measures of the sport is important.

What follows are a series of essays that I hope will demonstrate how hockey analysts can use reasoning and statistical tools to gain valuable insight into our game. Conventional thought is challenged in some and reinforced in others. Some of the work is economically important, sometimes it's done purely for fun—but it's always valuable, as long as it keeps us moving up the scale towards an ultimate understanding of hockey.

Chapter Three

Who's Good at the Draft?

Betting on the Future

Each June, NHL executives gather in an arena or convention center to place their bets on the future of hockey. The suits of the past season's worst teams pray to the hockey gods that the 18- to 20-year-old men they select in the draft will transform their franchises from laughingstocks into Stanley Cup contenders. Sometimes their prayers are answered, but for the most part they are ignored.

The inception of the league salary cap has increased the value of good drafting. NHL free-agency rules are designed in a way that makes young talent cheap. Freshly drafted players are bound by the NHL's collective bargaining agreement (CBA) to sign an "entry-level contract." This contract limits the salary and bonuses that can be paid to these young players. During Sidney

Crosby's entry-level contract period, which spanned three seasons from 2005 to 2008, he earned a salary of $850,000 annually. During that period, he had 99 goals and 195 assists. Over that same time span Marian Hossa was paid an average of $6 million annually, while scoring 111 goals and adding 147 assists. As you can see, it's far cheaper for a team to draft a Sidney Crosby than sign a Marian Hossa. Prior to the salary cap, teams didn't necessarily have to worry about absolute player costs. In the early 21st century, the New York Rangers and Toronto Maple Leafs used this strategy with little success. Under the current rules, success is dependent on getting more bang for the buck.

Besides the fact that they come cheap, another advantage to drafting and developing young players is realized when their entry-level contracts expire, sometime between the ages of 21 and 24. At this point, a player becomes a Group II restricted free agent. At the expiration of the initial contract, the team that drafted the player has the chance to match any offer from another team or else be compensated. For someone like Crosby, that compensation is four first-round draft picks. The obligation of other teams to compensate is good for the team that originally drafted the star player because the stipulation gives them a chance to keep the player they spent time scouting, drafting, developing and planning around. This practice is good for all NHL teams because it has the unintended consequence of putting a ceiling on (and possibly lowering) the salaries of all Group II free agents.

A Digression: Free Agency and Game Theory

Picture a world with perfect information—everybody knows exactly what something is worth in economic terms. In this perfect world, a loaf of bread is worth $1.50 because the ingredients cost $1.00, but the bread also provides $0.25 worth of nutritional value and $0.25 worth of culinary pleasure to the buyer. The price paid includes no hidden costs or benefits because the information we have is "perfect." Also in this world, Pittsburgh Penguin Sidney Crosby is a restricted free agent. The impotent Toronto Maple Leafs are considering making an offer. They have three options. The first is to offer Crosby a contract for precisely his economic value, which they know. If they do this, the Penguins will simply match the offer because they *also* know what Crosby is worth. Any rational team is willing to pay up to the true price of a player. The result: Crosby stays in Pittsburgh. The second choice the Maple Leafs have is to offer Crosby a contract below his known value. Once again, the Penguins need only present Crosby with a contract based on his true economic value. Because this contract offer will be higher in dollar terms than the Leafs' offer, Crosby will accept it and Toronto will be stymied again. The only other option Toronto has is to submit an offer to Crosby that's above his economic value. If they do this, Pittsburgh will allow Crosby to walk. Remember, this is a world where the exact economic value of Crosby is known. This value includes both the tangible and intangible things he brings to a team, from goal scoring to jersey sales to community appearances. Pittsburgh has no incentive to offer Crosby more than they know he's worth, so in our make-believe world, Toronto compensates Pittsburgh with draft picks—thanks to Group II free agency rules—and signs Crosby. However, this decision by the Leafs is completely irrational. They have no reason to pay more for Crosby than his true economic value, so offering Pittsburgh more than Crosby is worth makes absolutely no sense. Therefore, the best choice for the Maple Leafs is not to offer Crosby a contract at all. In a world of perfect information it goes against logic to do so because Toronto could never win Crosby without spending an amount that is beyond his true economic value. The end result in this NHL fantasyland is that Crosby stays in Pittsburgh and gets paid exactly what everyone knows he is worth.

This instance of second-guessing what each team will do in contract negotiations is an example of Game Theory. Game Theory is branch of mathematics that seeks to establish the outcomes of "games," or decisions made by entities when their courses of action are dependent on the choices of another party. In our example, there are two "players," the Pittsburgh Penguins and the Toronto Maple Leafs, participating in a game called "offer Sidney Crosby a contract." What each team does in the game depends on what the other decides to do. If Toronto offers a low contract, Pittsburgh matches it. If Toronto's offer is too high, they don't. Key to this game, however, is the idea of perfect information. In this case, since we know exactly what Crosby is worth, we can follow a chain of logical reasoning to arrive at the solution to the game: Sid stays in Pittsburgh. From a rational standpoint, no other outcome makes sense.

Back in the real world, the true economic value of a player is unknown. Despite this, teams are still required to consider the same factors that they would in the world of perfect information; they have to play the same "game." When Crosby's contract expires, should the

Maple Leafs make an offer or not? Toronto has the same options as before, but now has to consider the relative valuation of Crosby, rather than his true, unknown value. If Toronto values Crosby less than Pittsburgh does, the Leafs' offer will be matched by the Penguins. If Toronto values Crosby more than Pittsburgh does, the Penguins will forgo matching the contract and Crosby will sign with the Leafs. On the surface, this seems like a great outcome for the Maple Leafs. But the question Toronto management has to ask if they manage to sign Crosby is: did we overpay, or did Pittsburgh undervalue him?

Remember, in the world of perfect information, where we know Crosby's value, the only way the Maple Leafs can sign Crosby is if they intentionally overpay. Without perfect information, the Maple Leafs are only able to sign Crosby if a) they overpay, or b) Pittsburgh underestimates Crosby's value. In a two-team contract battle, it's easy to assume that your own team is correct when it comes to valuing a player's worth. After all, if you can't trust your own staff, who can you trust? But the confidence that your team is correct weakens as more teams enter the fray. Imagine 10 teams making contract bids on Crosby as a restricted free agent. No team knows what the others are bidding. You submit your bid, which is a proxy for what you think Crosby's true economic value is. Weeks later, you receive a call from Crosby's agent informing you that Crosby has agreed to sign with your team. Good, right? Well, consider that no team of the 10 that bid on Crosby knows exactly what his true value is, your team included. Yet each team does their best to estimate this value and submits that estimate as their contract offer. Since Crosby agrees to sign with your team, it follows that your bid was highest. Why, then, does every other team think Crosby is worth less than *you* believe he is? When the auction is between two teams, there's a good chance your estimated value is correct. But when you win a contract in a 10-team auction, there are nine other teams telling you you're paying too much money. They do this implicitly by proffering lower bids, believing Crosby to be worth less than the amount you submitted. In hindsight, how confident are you that you were right and the nine other teams were wrong? This is known as the Winner's Curse, which describes how the winner of an auction has likely overpaid for the asset.

One of the problems of the pre-salary-cap era was that high-revenue teams weren't punished for putting extremely high values on free agents. It was easy for these teams to throw money around willy-nilly. There were no repercussions for deliberately overbidding on Crosby, other than a smaller bottom line. In other words, teams with a big budget weren't particularly cursed by the Winner's Curse. But in a salary-cap world, where a dollar spent on one player is a dollar not spent somewhere else, the Winner's Curse might deter interested teams from bidding on free agents. These teams may decide that the "game" is unbeatable and that the only way they can win is by overpaying—an unfavorable option. This gives the free agent's original team a big advantage by limiting the competition of potential suitors.

How Much Is a Draft Pick Worth?

Another way in which the CBA's free-agency rules stack the deck in favor of a Group II player's team is in draft-pick compensation. Depending on the size of the contract tendered, the offering team has to give up draft picks if a Group II restricted free agent accepts their contract and changes teams. The higher the contract offer, the more picks the player's original team has to give up. If a team places a positive value on a draft pick, and I'd argue that they must, then that price has to be taken into consideration by the potential buyer when they're bidding on their desired free agent. To see how this favors the free agent's team, we'll return to our trusty analogy—the desperate Maple Leafs' bid to sign Sidney Crosby.

The Toronto executives put their eggheads on the case, and it is established that Crosby is worth $10 million annually over four years for a grand total of $40 million. The accountants also determine that the value of a first-round draft pick is $1 million. Since the projected offer to Crosby is so high, $10 million a year, the NHL free agency rules dictate that Toronto is on the hook for four first-round draft picks as compensation. Thus, the maximum contract they offer Crosby is the $40 million they believe he is worth, less the $4 million for the draft picks they would lose, for a total of $36 million. That's $9 million annually over four years. Pittsburgh crunches its own numbers and figures that Crosby is worth $9.5 million per year over the next four years, for a total of $38 million. Since the Maple Leafs' offer of $9 million per year is lower than the price the Penguins believe Crosby is worth, Pittsburgh will match Toronto's offer. However, the offer the Penguins must match is $2 million below what they really believe Crosby is worth, so they get a deal. This whole transaction occurs even though Toronto values Crosby more than the Penguins do. Therefore, Crosby's salary is potentially reduced, depending on how valuable teams believe draft picks are. For instance, imagine a scenario in which Toronto believes a draft pick is worth $5 million. Such a case would result in a maximum contract offer to Crosby of $20 million, or $5 million annually. Pittsburgh could match that offer easily and save a bundle, all thanks to Group II free agency rules meant to protect a team's home-grown assets.

Draft Results, 1995–2005

Clearly then, there are some huge advantages to drafting and developing talent rather than acquiring the equivalent talent via free agency. The system is rigged to give good drafting teams an advantage, first by forcing young players into cheap entry-level contracts and later by the contract matching/compensation process of Group II free agency. Under salary-cap constraints it's difficult to justify signing a team of free agents when equivalent, entry-level talent is much less expensive (recall Crosby versus Hossa). Of course, it's ridiculous to look at players like Crosby or Alexander Ovechkin—the most dominant rookies since Wayne Gretzky—as readily available, cheap talent. But the fact remains that in every draft year there are great players on tap. Here's a list of the top 10 forwards in their first or second year in the NHL in 2008–09, followed by the most high-profile free-agent forwards signed to contracts during 2008:

Rookies								
Player	Age	Team	G	A	P	GC	Salary	$/GC
Nicklas Backstrom	21	WAS	22	66	88	29.9	$850,000	$28,428.09
Jonathan Toews	20	CHI	34	35	69	27.3	$850,000	$31,135.53
Patrick Kane	20	CHI	25	45	70	25.2	$875,000	$34,722.22
Devin Setoguchi	22	SJS	31	34	65	25.1	$850,000	$33,864.54
Bobby Ryan	21	ANA	31	26	57	23.2	$850,000	$36,637.93
Bryan Little	21	ATL	31	20	51	22.3	$850,000	$38,116.59
Kris Versteeg	22	CHI	22	31	53	19.9	$490,000	$24,623.12
Patrik Berglund	20	STL	21	26	47	18.4	$850,000	$46,195.65
Steven Stamkos	18	TBL	23	23	46	18.3	$875,000	$47,814.21
Michael Frolik	20	FLA	21	24	45	17.8	$850,000	$47,752.81

Free Agents								
Player	Age	Team	G	A	P	GC	Salary	$/GC
Marian Hossa	30	DET	40	31	71	29.5	$7,450,000	$252,542.37
Kristian Huselius	30	CLB	21	35	56	20.9	$4,750,000	$227,272.73
Pavol Demitra	34	VAN	20	33	53	19.5	$4,000,000	$205,128.21
Ryan Malone	29	TBL	26	19	45	18.8	$4,250,000	$226,063.83
Markus Naslund	35	NYR	24	22	46	18.6	$4,000,000	$215,053.76
Vaclav Prospal	33	TBL	19	26	45	16.9	$3,500,000	$207,100.59
Miroslav Satan	34	PIT	17	19	36	14.2	$2,800,000	$197,183.10
Brian Rolston	35	NJD	15	17	32	12.4	$5,000,000	$403,225.81
Sergei Fedorov	39	WAS	11	22	33	12	$4,000,000	$333,333.33
Sean Avery	28	2Tm	8	14	22	7.9	$3,500,000	$443,037.97

Take a good look at the last column ($/GC), which puts a price on each player's offensive production. On a Goals Created basis, the top 10 free agents are nearly 10 times more expensive than the top 10 first- or second-year players. Since economics is all about finding efficiencies, the evidence suggests that teams might be better off putting time and money into drafting good players instead of signing them as free agents. With this in mind, I think it's an interesting experiment to look at which teams were most successful at the draft in recent years, and hence possibly keen to take advantage of this inefficiency.

The data I looked at covered the NHL Entry Drafts from 1995 to 2005. I figured that this time span was long enough to allow me to see which teams are significantly "better" at the draft than others. Using data up to 2005 ensured that the players drafted were at least given *some* time to make it to the NHL. Also, because of the time period of my data, I decided not to include Atlanta, Columbus, Nashville and Minnesota since these teams all entered the league post-1995.

To determine which teams, if any, are draft-savvy, I counted how many picks each team had during the decade of drafts. I then tabulated how many of those picks played at least one game in the NHL. Finally, I added up the total number of games in the NHL that the 1995–2005 draft picks have played in their careers. With this data, I calculated the Pick Rate, which is the percentage of players a team drafts who end up making the NHL, defined by play in at least one game. The two other metrics employed are Games Played per Pick and Games Played per NHL Pick. The first number indicates how many games played, on average, a team got out of each draft pick between 1995 and 2005. This gives us some idea of how good the team is, in general, at picking players. The second number tells us how many games played, on average, a team got from its draft picks who actually made the NHL. This is a proxy for the quality of the picks.

One major flaw with the methodology is that if a team drafts well in the early years of the data and poorly in the latter years, a team will appear "better" than another that drafts poorly in the early years and well later on. For example, a good draft pick from 1996 has had 13 seasons up until now to rack up NHL Games Played. Another equally skilled player, drafted in 2005, has only had three seasons of opportunity to play in NHL games. This problem can be resolved by normalizing the data or weighting old picks less than recent picks. However, I don't think this step is necessary. What I'm looking for is draft *ability*, which should be represented by a team's consistently successful picks. A team that continually makes good draft choices should also draft good players both early and late in the data and thus outperform other teams no matter what.

Besides, it's pretty easy to flip through the data to test the good early/good late hypothesis.

Another problem, though, is whether or not games played is a good indication of player skill and hence a team's draft-picking ability. I'll argue that while not perfect, games played is a pretty good indicator. First, it's a readily available statistic and everybody understands what it is. Second, a team's goal in the draft is to find NHL-caliber players. The objective isn't necessarily to find a Sidney Crosby or an Alexander Ovechkin, but to find players who deserve a roster spot and are therefore cheaper than an equivalent free agent. In this sense, games played works well; it measures a player's ability to maintain a roster spot. It's pretty hard to argue that a player who plays 1000 NHL games isn't "good." Finally, games played is easily applied across all positions. A good forward will play many games, as will a good defenseman or goalie.

Since this book is about questioning preconceived notions, I should talk about my own before we look at the data. If you asked me on the street which team is best at the draft, I would guess that Detroit has unbeatable drafting ability. And, having grown up watching the Maple Leafs, I'd guess they are in the running for the team with the worst drafting ability. Intuition tells me that good teams draft well, so I'd also expect the New Jersey Devils and the

Colorado Avalanche to be near the top of the rankings. The Devils, Avalanche and Red Wings won every Stanley Cup but two between 1995 and 2005. Other teams at the bottom of the list, in my opinion, would be perennial baddies like the Islanders and Rangers, and maybe the Blackhawks.

Here's the data:

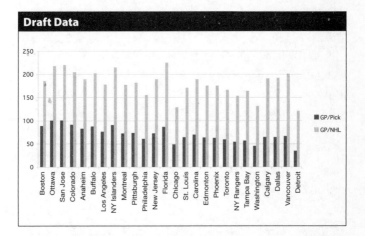

Draft Data						
Team	Picks	Made NHL	GP	Pick Rate	GP/Pick	GP/NHL
BOS	98	47	8717	0.48	88.95	185.47
OTT	102	47	10257	0.46	100.56	218.23
SJS	92	42	9263	0.46	100.68	220.55
COL	112	50	10256	0.45	91.57	205.12

Team	Picks	Made NHL	GP	Pick Rate	GP/Pick	GP/NHL
ANA	89	39	7384	0.44	82.97	189.33
BUF	106	46	9315	0.43	87.88	202.50
LAK	107	46	8186	0.43	76.50	177.96
NYI	102	43	9261	0.42	90.79	215.37
MTL	103	42	7467	0.41	72.50	177.79
PIT	106	43	7828	0.41	73.85	182.05
PHI	94	37	5748	0.39	61.15	155.35
NJD	109	42	7959	0.39	73.02	189.50
FLA	104	40	9013	0.38	86.66	225.33
CHI	121	46	5936	0.38	49.06	129.04
STL	98	37	6341	0.38	64.70	171.38
CAR	92	34	6443	0.37	70.03	189.50
EDM	113	41	7196	0.36	63.68	175.51
PHX	95	34	5960	0.36	62.74	175.29
TOR	98	35	5841	0.36	59.60	166.89
NYR	110	39	5987	0.35	54.43	153.51
TBL	112	39	6406	0.35	57.20	164.26
WAS	104	36	4739	0.35	45.57	131.64
CGY	106	36	6886	0.34	64.96	191.28
DAL	104	35	6731	0.34	64.72	192.31
VAN	96	32	6429	0.33	66.97	200.91
DET	97	28	3392	0.29	34.97	121.14

Draft Data cont.

According to these results, sorted by Pick Rate, Boston is the most efficient team at picking NHL-caliber players, with 48 percent of the Bruins' picks making the NHL. Boston is followed closely by Ottawa and San Jose (46 percent) and Colorado (45 percent). The teams at the bottom are Calgary and Dallas, whose draft picks only made the NHL at a rate of 34 percent, followed by Vancouver at 33 percent. And the worst team? My preliminary pick for the best, Detroit. The Red Wings had the smallest proportion of draft picks make the NHL between 1995 and 2005, only 29 percent.

I don't think I'm alone in my surprise at the results of the Detroit Red Wings in the data. Not only does the team perform poorly in the Pick Rate metric, but when we look at how many games, on average, one of their draft picks who actually makes the NHL plays (yes, that's an unfortunate mouthful), the Red Wings finish dead last again, at 121.14 Games Played per NHL Pick. This means that when Detroit manages to select a player good enough to make it into the NHL, that player is generally not as "good" (doesn't play as many games) as a draft selection from another team. Since these results are a slap in the face to intuition, they warrant a closer look.

The Detroit Red Wings: Legend or Myth?

Much of the legend surrounding Detroit's amazing drafting ability rests on the shoulders of three players. In the seventh round of the 1999 entry draft, the Red Wings drafted a young Swede by the name of Henrik Zetterberg. In his rookie season in 2002–03, Zetterberg scored 22 goals and 22 assists, earning 18.2 Goals Created. He's improved in nearly every season since, averaging nearly 26 Goals Created over his six-year career. Zetterberg also gets attention for his defensive play, earning a Selke Trophy nomination in 2008. Calling Zetterberg a good seventh-rounder is an understatement.

Detroit did even better the previous year when the team drafted Pavel Datsyuk in the sixth round, 171st overall. Datsyuk took a few seasons to warm up but has since established himself as a top-tier NHL forward. He has averaged 26.3 Goals Created per season over his career, scoring 171 goals and 351 assists. He's made three NHL all-star teams, won three Lady Byng Trophies as the league's most sportsmanlike player and won the Selke Trophy as the NHL's best defensive forward in 2008. In other words, for a sixth-round pick, Detroit ended up with a spectacular bargain.

But Detroit's drafting heroics didn't begin there. In the third round of the 1989 NHL Entry Draft the Red Wings snagged defenseman Nicklas Lidstrom. Lidstrom has had an amazing NHL career. Some of his achievements include four Stanley Cups, 10 All-Star games, six Norris

Trophies as the NHL's top defenseman and one Conn Smyth Trophy. He is one of only 22 players in the world to have won a Stanley Cup, an Olympic gold medal and an IIHF World Championship. With 997 career points, he's 74th on the all-time scoring list, averaging 19.6 Goals Created over his 17-year career. Lidstrom has also averaged more than 27 minutes per game since the NHL started tracking ice time in 1998, including 24 minutes per game in 2008–09 as a 39-year-old. I think it's safe to say that Nick Lidstrom was a solid third-round pick for Detroit.

And so the argument goes that these players (Zetterberg, Datsyuk and Lidstrom) are indicative of the Red Wings' ability to dig diamonds from the dirt, obtaining value from their late-round picks. But I'm not sure this argument makes sense when I look at it more closely. If I owned the Detroit franchise and my general manager told me he was going to give opposing teams 52 opportunities to select a player like Lidstrom, who will end up retiring as one of the best defensemen of all time, I'd probably have a heart attack. Why would you deliberately *wait* to draft such a player? The idea is absurd. There's no point in taking that risk, and any manager who purposely used that strategy might have an eye for talent but he completely lacks common sense. Picking a player like Lidstrom in the third round, rather than the first, knowing how good he would eventually be, is irresponsible. The same can be said of the late-round selections of Zetterberg and Datsyuk. In 1999, the Wings drafted three players ahead of Zetterberg, only one of whom made the NHL (Kent McDonell, who played 32 career games with Columbus). Detroit drafted *seven* players before Datsyuk in 1998, including one prior to him in the same round. Of these seven players, only two made the NHL. One was Jiri Fischer, selected in the first round, 25th overall. He was a solid defenseman who played with the team until he had a heart attack on the bench in 2005. The other player, Ryan Barnes, played a grand total of four minutes in the league.

The problem is, other than Zetterberg, Datsyuk and Lidstrom, Detroit hasn't done anything particularly brilliant as far as the draft is concerned. Admittedly, they've found a few solid defenders in Niklas Kronwell (2000) and Kyle Quincey (2003), who now plays for the Los Angeles Kings. Other notable players drafted by Detroit are Johan Franzen (2004), Valtteri Filppula (2002) and Jiri Hudler (2002)—all solid picks but not household names outside the Motor City. In between are swaths of unrecognizable players who never get any more than a cup of coffee in the NHL. If Detroit is as good as we think they are, shouldn't they be able to pick at least one NHL-caliber player every year?

One argument that might curry Detroit some favor is that their dominance during the period I've selected has stuck them with late-round draft positions. There is some truth to this, though it doesn't seem to have caused a problem for other good teams during the era, mainly New Jersey and Colorado. Still, maybe Detroit's drafting skills allow them to outperform teams in the later rounds. One way to see if there's any merit to this is to compare the Red Wings' Pick Rate, by round, with the league average:

Red Wings Pick Rate		
Round	Detroit	League
2	73%	60%
3	67%	48%
4	27%	32%
5	7%	25%
6	20%	26%
7	20%	24%
8	9%	25%
9	10%	22%

The Red Wings have slightly outperformed the league average Pick Rate in the second and third rounds, but have underachieved, sometimes drastically, in rounds four through nine. I wouldn't draw any hard and fast conclusions from this simple analysis, but I don't see anything compelling enough to say that Detroit is any *better* than the average team at picking players in the late rounds.

I'm not trying to take anything away from Detroit as a franchise. They've proven they know how to build teams to win championships. But I think we tend to believe that a good franchise is great at everything, and therefore Detroit must also draft well. As evidence of this, we point to the amazing players they managed to grab in the late rounds of the draft. Yet there is more than one way to build a winning team. One team might commit to scouting, drafting and developing players. Another might find its strength through quality free-agent signings and smart trades. Other teams might use a combination of both. Keep in mind that prior to the salary cap, Detroit was a high-budget team that didn't *need* to draft well. They may have figured out something that the New York Rangers and Toronto Maple Leafs couldn't—how to spend money but win at the same time.

This analysis is certainly not reason enough to completely condemn the Red Wings as a bad drafting team, but it achieves what I wanted it to, and that is for us to, at the very least, question the legend.

The Others

Now let's turn our attention away from Detroit and look at some other interesting draft results. Just as expected, the Maple Leafs and the Rangers are near the bottom of the 26-team list, placing 20th and 21st, respectively. Chicago, on the other hand, has its own unique style of draft incompetence. Over the decade I chose to sample from, the Blackhawks had more draft picks (121) than any other team. Their Pick Rate of 38 percent was only slightly below the league average of 39 percent, and the number of games played by their players that made it to the NHL was second lowest overall. This result makes sense when you think about it a little harder. Chicago floundered at the bottom of the league standings, but they were able to put many of their draft picks into the lineup (i.e., these picks made the NHL according to my stipulations of them playing in at least one game). This inflated Chicago's Pick Rate enough that it almost reached the league average. However, the players picked weren't that great, as demonstrated by the low GP/NHL Pick statistic (this also shows us why it's important to look at more than one measure when analyzing our hockey data).

As for the New York Islanders, they might be the perfect example of a team that was good early in the draft sample, but bad later on. According to my metrics, the Islanders have an above-average Pick Rate of 42 percent. The Islanders also place fourth in the GP/NHL Pick category, which, combined with their Pick Rate, indicates that the players the Islanders pick who make the NHL are all pretty good. But here's a breakdown of the team's Pick Rate before and after 2000:

Islanders Pick Rate			
	Picks	Made NHL	Pick Rate
1995–99	52	28	0.54
2000–05	50	15	0.30

Ouch. You can expect a slight discrepancy between the two time periods because players drafted between 1995 and 1999 have had longer to develop, but the numbers here are still pretty significant. They also explain why the Islanders appear so high in the overall rankings. The way my analysis is structured, it will reward inconsistent teams that just happen to draft better in the earlier years of the sample. What it doesn't explain, however, is why the New York Islanders went from drafting well to drafting poorly. My answer? Charles Wang.

The Islanders of the mid-1990s were mired in ownership controversy. John Pickett, who owned the team during its dynasty years of the early 1980s, was actively shopping the team. In 1996, it appeared he had found a buyer in Dallas businessman John Spano. Months after the deal for the team closed, it was discovered that Spano was a fraud; he had misled Pickett and the NHL about his wealth and had forged documents relating to the sale. Spano was consequently convicted and sentenced to five years in prison.

Pickett eventually found another buyer, an ownership group led by a co-owner of the Phoenix Coyotes. The deal fell apart, however, when the potential buyers refused to purchase the team without certification that the Islanders' home arena was safe. Pickett, knowing the arena was in disrepair, refused to get the certification, and the deal collapsed.

Throughout the controversy, GM Mike Milbury was seemingly able to draft solid players. As the data shows, he had a solid record from 1995 to 1999. In fact, between 1995 and 1999, only three of his first five picks in each round failed to make the NHL. His 1999 draft was particularly successful, with nine of 14 picks making the big league. But in 2000, the team was sold to Computer Associates founder Charles Wang. Wang was known as a loose cannon in the corporate world. He was a takeover machine who swooped in and bought companies, then mercilessly fired their top management.

Wang has made it clear that he is the one who makes the decisions when it comes to the Islanders. He's also made it clear that he doesn't know a whole lot about the business of hockey. For starters, he bought the New York Islanders (zing!). Further, Wang made the news in 2006 after he signed Rick DiPietro to a 15-year contract and one of the laziest but most talented players, Alexei Yashin, to a 10-year contract. In that same season, he fired Neil Smith—the GM responsible for building the 1994 Stanley Cup-winning Rangers—after Smith had been on the job for only 40 days. It was reported that this firing was because of philosophical differences. Apparently, Smith couldn't understand why Wang needed to have a say in everything, including the hiring of the team's equipment manager. But the story gets even more ridiculous. To replace Smith, Wang hired Garth Snow, who at the time was only 35 years old, had zero executive NHL experience and was the team's backup goalie.

Snow might yet turn out to be a good NHL general manager, but Wang's selection of him is still a bit odd. And knowing what we do now about Wang and his hands-on micromanagement style, it's hard to imagine that he didn't have an influence on the team's draft picks between 2000 and 2005. My theory might be wrong, but it does explain how the Isles outperformed the average

Pick Rate during the first five years of my data and miserably underperformed during the last five years. The point is, the team's draft-picking ability probably isn't as good the metric tells us it is.

Are the Good Teams any Good?

Let's take a look at the data again and see if *any* of the teams with high Pick Rates truly display good drafting ability. Once again, a team that has talent at drafting should be able to consistently outperform the rest of the league. What follows are graphs that represent how each of the top-five Pick Rate teams did in each draft of the sample 10 years, relative to the rest of the league. Where the line is above zero, the team outperformed the league average Pick Rate for the corresponding season:

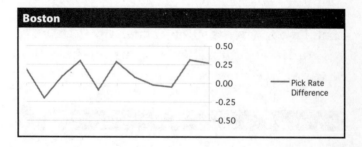

The team with the highest Pick Rate, the Boston Bruins, is a model of inconsistency over the sample. The Bruins alternate between over- and underperforming versus the league average between 1995 and 2005. Fortunately for them, their overperformances are stronger than their underperformances. However, there doesn't appear to be any real reason to believe that Boston management has figured out a surefire drafting strategy.

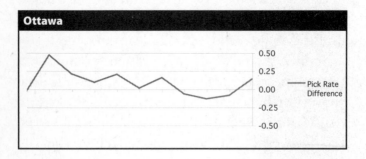

The Ottawa Senators look like they did extremely well early in the sample of drafts, beating the league average for six straight seasons, 1996 to 2001. After that, for a few years, Ottawa fares worse than the rest of the league. There is nothing here that screams, "We know how to draft!"

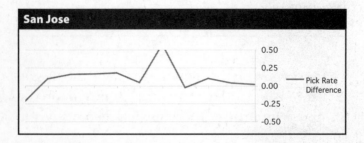

San Jose, on the other hand, looks like they may be onto something. After 1995, a year in which fewer of their picks made the NHL when compared to the rest of the league, the Sharks go six years at a better-than-average clip, including one year (2001) when every single draft pick made the NHL. After slightly underperforming in 2002, San Jose proceeded to do better than the rest of the NHL for the remaining years in the data sample. With the caveat that we are drawing conclusions from a small sample, San Jose might be a good example of a team that has realized the value of drafting well.

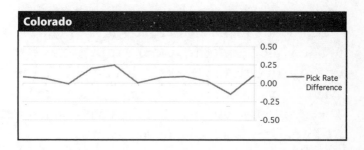

The Colorado Avalanche is another team that appears to have drafting ability. The Avalanche does better than the rest of the league in eight of 11 drafts in the sample. In the three other seasons, Colorado hovers at the league average, underperforming only in 2004. Most surprising is that the Avalanche was a dominant team over the sample, perhaps putting to rest the idea that good teams like Detroit can't draft as well as "bad" teams because of draft position. If we look at the stats, over the 10-year sample period, Colorado won two Stanley Cups, nine division titles and averaged 102 points per season.

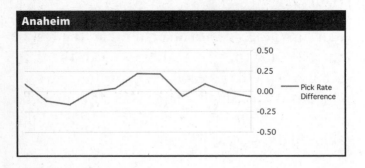

Anaheim's high Pick Rate appears attributable to a few good drafts around the turn of the 21st century. In fact, the Ducks only outperform the league average in five of the 11 drafts in the sample. The highs outdo the lows, but there's no evidence that Anaheim is a great drafting team.

Conclusions

Drafting and developing talent is a sure way to get a leg up on the competition, thanks to regulations established by the NHL's CBA. The concept of my little analysis here was to see if there are any teams that, realizing the value and importance of the draft, have established a method of finding NHL-ready talent. Now that you've seen the data, what does it really tell us?

First, it's important to realize that no rigid conclusions can be drawn, and this is because of the relatively small sample size—11 drafts. It's very possible that a team could outperform the league average based on pure luck. Also, the difference separating a team that drafts better than the league average versus a team that drafts worse sometimes comes down to only one player making (or not making) the NHL. That's not much leeway.

On the other hand, it doesn't make much sense to expand the sample to 20 or 30 years and, based on that data, proclaim that one team or another has a good draft "system." The NHL game changed dramatically over that period, as did amateur hockey and the entire management of NHL teams. How much do the Red Wings of 1980 have in common with the team of today? Different owners, different management and certainly different draft strategies do not the same team make.

Keeping that in mind, what conclusions *can* we draw from recent draft history? I think it's evident that teams aren't as good or as bad at drafting as we believe they are. The sign of a decent metric is that it will not only validate assumptions but also reveal some surprises. Pick Rate, while definitely not perfect, does this. Teams like the Toronto Maple Leafs and the New York Rangers fare poorly, whereas the San Jose Sharks and the Colorado Avalanche come out looking good. Intuition tells us that Detroit is one of the best and the Islanders one of the worst; the metric, as we saw, disagrees.

Based on this evidence, I conclude that few teams, if any, have the actual "ability" to pick outstanding players in the draft year after year. In fact, I might go so far as to say that the NHL draft is a total crapshoot. There is a vast amount of luck involved with projecting the physical, mental and emotional development of an 18-year-old hockey player. Of course, that doesn't mean NHL management should ignore the annual entry draft, dismissing it as unpredictable. As I said, the availability of cheap talent is far too important for that. Instead, the teams should try and find a way to do better because it appears there is too much talent and money being left on the table.

Chapter Four

Crosby versus Ovechkin

Choosing Between Champions

It's probably the hockey argument of this generation: which player would you rather have on your team, the Pittsburgh Penguins' Sidney Crosby or the Washington Capitals' Alexander Ovechkin? We've heard the this-player-or-that-player debate before. During the late 1980s, it was popular to discuss the relative merits of Mario Lemieux and Wayne Gretzky. Unfortunately, except for a few seasons, the players were difficult to compare directly. Gretzky was well into his NHL career by the time Lemieux came into the picture, and Lemieux was plagued with injuries from the middle of his career onwards. The Gretzky versus Lemieux dispute was intriguing, but fans were usually left with an unsatisfying resolution.

The circumstances surrounding Crosby and Ovechkin make for a much more appealing player debate. For instance, despite being drafted first overall in consecutive years, thanks to the NHL lockout, both players made their debut in 2005. And, barring a catastrophic injury, we're likely to see these players age together, peak together and face each other many times over the course of their careers. It's Canada versus Russia. Flamboyancy versus modesty. Playmaking vision versus raw goal-scoring ability. It's the stuff of hockey dreams. But who is the better player?

The Past

In determining who is better, it's sensible to examine how Crosby and Ovechkin have performed up to the most recent point in their careers. We'll start the comparison looking backwards. Here's what their rookie seasons looked like:

Rookie Season								
	GP	G	A	P	+/-	PIM	Shots	ATOI
Alexander Ovechkin	81	52	54	106	2	52	425	21:37
Sidney Crosby	81	39	63	102	-1	110	278	20:08

Both young players, living up to expectations in their first year in the NHL, had surprisingly similar seasons. Ovechkin showed that he had no problem scoring in the league, burying 52 goals, good for third place overall in the NHL in 2005–06.

Crosby was no slouch, either, racking up 39 goals of his own. Taking their goal totals and Goals Created (Ovechkin, 43.9; Crosby, 37.4) into account, the player with the rookie-year edge is probably Ovechkin. Lo and behold, hockey journalists agreed, awarding Ovie the Calder Trophy as the league's rookie of the year.

The 2006–07 season was Crosby's turn to shine:

2006–07	GP	G	A	P	+/–	PIM	SOG	ATOI
Alexander Ovechkin	82	46	46	92	-19	52	392	21:23
Sidney Crosby	79	36	84	120	10	60	250	20:46

Ovechkin had another great year, finishing fourth in the league in goals. But Crosby was dominant, leading the league in points per game and Goals Created per game. Riding on the shoulders of Crosby, the Pittsburgh Penguins climbed out of their division basement for the first time in five years. Crosby also scored a hat trick at the 2007 NHL awards show, winning the Art Ross, Hart and Lester B. Pearson trophies. So, after tremendous rookie years, with Ovie taking the first round, the sophomore-season scale tips back the other way, placing Sid the Kid at the forefront.

In the 2007–08 season, Washington's star came out swinging like a boxer against the ropes, knocking out his best performance to date. Ovechkin, helped out because Crosby injured himself and was limited to only 53 games that season, ended up on top.

2007–08								
	GP	G	A	P	+/-	PIM	SOG	ATOI
Alexander Ovechkin	82	65	47	112	28	40	446	23:06
Sidney Crosby	53	24	48	72	18	39	173	20:51

Ovechkin also cleaned up at the 2008 NHL awards, capturing the Art Ross, Lester B. Pearson, Hart and Maurice Richard trophies, outdoing Crosby's previous performance in 2007. But let's not be too hasty in giving away the 2007–08 season to Ovie. A closer examination of Ovechkin and Crosby reveals that on a per game basis, the players were a lot closer than their counting statistics tell us. Ovechkin slightly edged out Sid in points per game, 1.37 to 1.36, but Crosby led the league in assists per game with 0.91, and should also get a bit of credit for helping his team reach the Stanley Cup finals. Still, we can't ignore the fact that Ovechkin was brilliant that season. Ovie therefore takes the round after the end of the two stars' third NHL season.

The 2008–09 season saw Ovechkin and Crosby finish second and third overall, respectively, in the league's scoring race, behind Crosby's teammate Evgeni Malkin:

2008–09								
	GP	G	A	P	+/–	PIM	SOG	ATOI
Alexander Ovechkin	79	56	54	110	8	72	528	22:31
Sidney Crosby	77	33	70	103	3	76	237	21:56

Ovechkin led the league in goals once again, also beating Crosby in points per game (1.39 to 1.34) and Goals Created (45.2 to 36.4). Crosby was good, but I think Ovechkin was slightly better.

What I wanted to point out here was just how close Crosby and Ovechkin are and to showcase their four great seasons in the league. Let's look now at the career totals of these two able young guns:

Career Totals									
	GP	G	A	P	+/–	PIM	Shots	ATOI	PPG	GC/G
Alexander Ovechkin	324	219	201	420	19	216	1791	22:02	1.30	0.54
Sidney Crosby	290	132	265	397	30	285	938	20:32	1.37	0.49

It's hard to take anything away from either of these players because both are superb. Ovechkin is clearly the better goal scorer, but Crosby earned more points on a per game basis, and did so playing, per game, about two minutes less than Ovechkin. When put up against Crosby's 29 missed games in 2007–08, Ovechkin comes out as the more durable player, but Crosby closed that gap by doubling the total of Ovechkin's career post-season games played.

So, Crosby or Ovechkin? Making a decision based on their careers up to this point is incredibly difficult. If you twisted my arm and forced me to choose, I'd probably take Ovechkin, but I wouldn't be the slightest bit disappointed if you shoved Crosby down my throat instead. Not really an answer, is it? It seems that if we want to end this debate, one of two things needs to happen: we can wait for these two players to retire, or we can try to predict the future.

The Future

Describing the projection of a hockey player's career as "difficult" is an understatement. The number of things that can derail a career are nearly infinite. Maybe it's a catastrophic injury just as a player enters his prime. Perhaps a 17-year-old prospect being scouted turns out to be a little unstable. The array of problems a player might face is tough to foresee, but, somewhat impossibly, predicting how players are likely to perform in the future is vital to constructing a team. This vision in the crystal ball is also important to all the armchair general managers of the world who want to know whether the Penguins or the Capitals got the best man. In order to answer this question, we need a model that tells us what an NHL career looks like.

Ken Kryzwicki decided that the best method of defining an NHL career curve was to ignore the outliers and examine what the average NHL career looks like. Starting with the 2005–06 season, he gathered data on players in the league with at least 10 years of NHL service. There were 160 players who fit Kryzwicki's criteria. He then broke down each player's point totals into cumulative percentage of points, by years of service. For example, a specific player might have earned 10 percent of his career points by year two of his career, 60 percent by year five and 99 percent by year eight. After calculating this breakdown for each of the 160 players in his study, Kryzwicki plotted the data and fit it with a model.

A major insight of Kryzwicki's career-curve framework is that the starting age of a young NHLer matters. Players who start in the NHL at a later age tend to peak earlier and have shorter careers.

Kryzwicki found that there were three significant lines in the sand: players who started their
career before age 20, those who started at age 20
or 21 and those whose careers began after the
age of 22. The data revealed that after 10 years,
the average NHL player who entered the league
before age 20 was only at 70 percent of total point
production, whereas a player who started in the
NHL later than age 22 was at 80 percent. There is
an intuitive argument to this discovery. Generally, the better a player is, the easier time he'll
have breaking into the league at a young age.
Better players should also perform the most consistently, as well as stick around the league longer
since their "decline years" are usually less drastic
than those of a more modestly talented player
who entered the league at a later age. The beauty
of Kryzwicki's career-curve model comes from
the quantification of this effect.

The age factor is relevant in our argument
because Crosby, who broke into the league as
an 18-year-old, has a two-year advantage over
Ovechkin. According to Kryzwicki's career-curve
model, Crosby should have a slightly better
career projection.

There are, however, some problems with using
the model to predict how Ovechkin's and Crosby's
careers will pan out. For one, we're looking at

two of the best hockey players the NHL has seen in a long time. It's possible that an exceptional hockey player's career doesn't play out the same way the average NHLer's does. There's also the issue of aggregating data, finding the average and using it to predict the career of an individual. There's a lot of room for error. Of course, the counter-argument is simple: what is the alternative? I've stressed the importance of being able to predict the future per-formance of a hockey player. Kryzwicki's model provides a quantitative method for doing that, and is likely to outperform anyone's best guess, including the opinions of the so-called experts. Therefore, despite the problems, I'll put my money on the data.

So, better career—Crosby or Ovechkin? Accord-ing to Kryzwicki's data, a player who started his career before age 20 earned, on average, 22.77 per-cent of his career points after his fourth year in the league. This pertains to Crosby. For players like Ovechkin, who began their journey at age 20, the average point accumulation was 23.69. Assuming that the model might miss its point projection by 10 percent, here are the career estimates for the two players:

Career Estimates			
	Career Points to Date	High Est.	Low Est.
Alexander Ovechkin	420	1950	1596
Sidney Crosby	397	1918	1569

Wow, those numbers are astonishingly close! Although Crosby is behind Ovechkin now, using Kryzwicki's model, Sid the Kid is projected to possibly end up pulling ahead of Ovie closer to the stars' retirement, thanks to Crosby's original age advantage when he entered the NHL. You can draw two conclusions from this result:

1) Using Kryzwicki's data, both players are projected to have amazing NHL careers.

2) It's impossible to determine whose career will be better.

And so we end the discussion much like it began. It's the argument of our age: Alexander Ovechkin or Sidney Crosby? I think hockey fans should consider themselves blessed that both players have lived up to their hype. And although we'd love to have an answer to the question of who is actually the better player, neither looking at past performances nor using quantitative measures to anticipate the future is going to give it to us. We'll just have to wait.

Chapter Five

Which Teams Spend Wisely?

Many sports fans consider it a sacrilege to talk about their favorite team as a business, but the reality is most major-league teams, including those of the NHL, are owned by business people first, sports fans second. Although teams might incur some financial losses in order to build a fan base or short-term winning strategy, a team that consistently loses money can't survive. This intersection of money and our beloved game diminishes a bit of the innocence most casual fans associate with playing hockey. Beyond the action on the ice, we have witnessed contract disputes, strikes and lockouts and talk of greedy players and owners—all over a game.

Fortunately, team owners and fans agree on the most important aspect of professional sport: everyone wants to see their team win games. To hockey lovers, there isn't anything much more exciting than seeing their home team compete for the

Stanley Cup. And all else being equal, more wins mean more revenues for the owners. For them, winning the maximum amount of games for the minimum cost is the ultimate goal.

So, an important question to ask from both a business person's and fan's perspective is: which NHL teams are best at spending money on winning games? I decided to examine some recent seasons and see which teams are most efficient at spending money to do just that.

Pythagorean Theorem Revisited

Up to this point in the book we've operated under the assumption that scoring and preventing goals is the key to winning hockey games. But now we can do better—we can prove it.

Once again, a Bill James formula, developed for baseball but adapted to hockey, is the tool of choice. James' Pythagorean Expectation formula estimates how many wins a team should accumulate based on its total goals for and goals against. The formula is:

$$\text{Expected Wins} = ((\text{Goals For})^2 / ((\text{Goals For})^2 + (\text{Goals Against})^2)) * \text{Games Played}$$

For a team that scores 250 goals and allows 200 over an NHL season, the calculation is:

$$\text{Expected Wins} = (250^2 / (250^2 + 200^2)) * 82$$

So, the expected wins of such a team are 50. The formula is elegantly simple—just a manipulation of the trigonometry formula taught in grade school—and surprisingly accurate at predicting a team's winning percentage. Here's a graph of expected versus actual wins for a sample containing data from all teams in the 2003–04 and 2008–09 seasons:

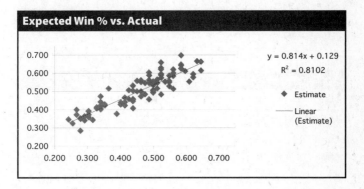

Each point on the graph represents a team, with their actual winning percentage on the horizontal axis and the Pythagorean estimate of their win percentage, based on goals for and against, on the vertical axis. If the formula was perfect, each point would form part of a perfectly straight line and the formula would predict, say, a 0.500 win percentage for a team that actually won games at a 0.500 rate. What's shown here isn't perfect, but it's close.

Over this small sample, the predictions look pretty good, but they're even better over the long run. Alan Ryder plotted the same graph for all NHL seasons between 1946 and 2003 and found that over 90 percent of a team's actual winning percentage was explained through the Pythagorean Expectation formula of goals for and against. The formula is so accurate, in fact, that analysts have come to explain deviations from the prediction as "luck." The following table is from the 2008–09 season:

2008–09					
Team	GF	GA	Act. Win %	Ex. Win %	Diff.
ANA	245	238	0.512	0.514	-0.002
ATL	257	280	0.427	0.457	-0.030
BOS	274	196	0.646	0.662	-0.015
BUF	250	234	0.500	0.533	-0.033
CAR	254	248	0.561	0.512	0.049
CGY	239	226	0.549	0.528	0.021
CHI	264	216	0.561	0.599	-0.038
CLB	199	257	0.390	0.375	0.015
COL	226	230	0.500	0.491	0.009
DAL	230	257	0.439	0.445	-0.006
DET	295	244	0.622	0.594	0.028
EDM	234	248	0.463	0.471	-0.008
FLA	234	231	0.500	0.506	-0.006
LAK	207	234	0.415	0.439	-0.024
MIN	219	200	0.488	0.545	-0.057
MTL	249	247	0.500	0.504	-0.004

2008–09 cont.					
Team	GF	GA	Act. Win %	Ex. Win %	Diff.
NAS	213	233	0.488	0.455	0.033
NJD	244	209	0.622	0.577	0.045
NYI	201	279	0.317	0.342	-0.025
NYR	210	218	0.524	0.481	0.043
OTT	217	237	0.439	0.456	-0.017
PHI	264	238	0.537	0.552	-0.015
PHX	208	252	0.439	0.405	0.034
PIT	264	239	0.549	0.550	-0.001
SJS	257	204	0.646	0.613	0.033
STL	233	233	0.500	0.500	0.000
TBL	210	279	0.293	0.362	-0.069
TOR	250	293	0.415	0.421	-0.007
VAN	246	220	0.549	0.556	-0.007
WAS	272	245	0.610	0.552	0.058

The fourth and fifth columns represent the 2008 teams' actual winning percentage and the win percentage predicted by the formula. The sixth column is the difference between the two. Pythagoras doesn't miss by more than seven percent on any estimate. According to the data, Tampa Bay, Minnesota and Chicago were the unluckiest teams last season. We consider them to have bad luck because the Pythagorean formula predicts more wins than they actually obtained. Interestingly, all three of the teams' seasons ended under completely different circumstances.

The Lightning were horrible, winning barely more than one-quarter of their games. Pythagoras predicts that the Lightning should have won 36 percent of their games, when they actually only won 29 percent.

The Minnesota Wild, on the other hand, were in a battle with Anaheim for the final playoff spot in the Western Conference. The Wild ended up losing the spot by three points. However, their Win Expectation—nearly four wins higher than what they actually achieved—would have easily put them into the playoffs.

Chicago had a fantastic season, and Pythagoras says it could have been even better. But good enough to surpass division-leading Detroit? Probably not.

The three luckiest teams were Washington, New Jersey and Carolina. These teams displayed their good luck by winning more games than their goals for and against predicted. Both Washington and New Jersey handily won their respective division titles, so their luck didn't really come into play in the standings. But Carolina went on a late-season surge to clinch a playoff spot by four points. Somewhere along the line the Hurricanes snagged four wins more than what their Win Expectation gave them. Good luck put them into the playoffs.

(In case you're wondering how to convert the percentages into wins, you multiply the percentage by 82, the number of games in a season. The Carolina Hurricanes outperformed the Win Expectation formula by 0.049, so 0.049 * 82 is 4.018, or approximately four wins.)

As interesting as examining over- and under-performers is, there's a more important purpose to the analysis. Pythagorean Win Expectation demonstrates that winning hockey games is predictable. A team merely needs to score many goals and allow few. Hence, a smart owner should spend his money in exactly that manner. Do NHL owners actually do that?

Spending it Wisely?

Based on what we've learned so far—that goals for and against accurately predict wins—a logical assumption is that the teams with the highest payrolls score the most goals, allow the fewest goals or both. Teams want to win games, and Pythagoras shows that there is a way to do so. Implicit in this assumption, however, is that teams choose to spend money as efficiently as possible on areas—scoring and preventing goals—that help the team. Using regression analysis we can look at teams' payrolls, goals for and goals against to see if money is truly being spent where it will help win games.

Regression analysis is a statistical method that allows us to examine the relationship between a dependent variable and one (or more) independent variable. In this case, we want to look at the relationship between goals for and payroll in one instance, and goals against in the other. We'll start with data from the 2003–04 season. Here's a graph of the data, plotting teams by goals for and payroll:

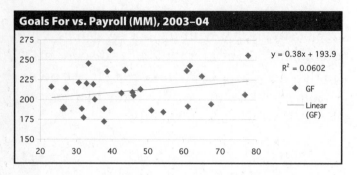

Each point on the graph represents a team, the horizontal axis is the total team payroll in millions and the vertical axis is the number of goals scored by the team. Recall we hypothesized that teams with high payrolls would score a lot of goals. Is that what you see in the graph? It's pretty hard to tell. However, the black line, called the linear estimate, can help us out. The line is estimated by linear regression and acts as a "best fit" trend line. It's telling us that there is a general upward trend in the data, just as we expected. As payroll increases, teams score more goals.

Looking at the individual points on the graph tells a slightly different story. It's difficult to determine the trend without the regression line. The points are literally all over the map. For example, both the highest- and lowest-scoring teams have the same payroll—about $36 million. So although we can determine the trend mathematically, it's difficult to detect visually.

Fortunately, statistics provides us with another measurement that enables us to deal with such an unobvious trend. That statistic is the correlation coefficient, represented by "rho." Rho gives us a measure of the "strength" of the relationship between our two variables: goals for and payroll. Positive relationships are represented by values of rho between 0 and 1, with the relationship "strengthening" as the number increases. If rho is between –1 and 0 it indicates a negative relationship, with –1 being the "strongest." In the previous analysis, the correlation coefficient rho is 0.24, representing a weak, positive relationship between our variables.

Let's take it a step further. When the correlation coefficient metric is squared, we obtain the coefficient of determination, represented by R-squared and shown in the previous graph. The coefficient of determination tells us how good our model—in the aforementioned case, that payroll determines goals for—is at prediction. Values of R-squared can fall anywhere between 0 and 1 (thanks to the fact that these values are the square of rho, which falls between –1 and 1). The specific value of R-squared for this relationship is 0.0602. That's a tiny number. Formally, it says that about six percent of the variation in a team's goals for is explained by the team's payroll. Putting statistical jargon aside, the low R-squared value explains numerically what was easily determined by looking at the graph: there might be a relationship between the variables, but it's weak.

So what does this mean for us? Loosely, when teams spend money they aren't spending it all trying to acquire "goals for." In fact, a very small proportion of their spending goes toward getting goals. That's odd, considering how important goals are for winning games. Perhaps, then, they are spending money in an attempt to prevent goals? When we perform the same analysis on goals against and payroll for the 2003–04 season, we get:

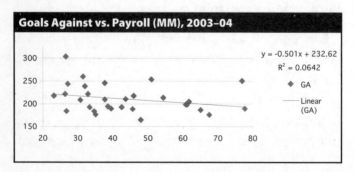

Goals Against vs. Payroll (MM), 2003–04

$y = -0.501x + 232.62$
$R^2 = 0.0642$

◆ GA

—— Linear (GA)

Once again, the points are scattered about the graph, making it difficult to precisely determine the trend by eye alone. The linear estimate for goals against and payroll slopes slightly downward, with an R-squared value of 0.0642 (rho=−0.25). That's another weak relationship, indicating that teams didn't do the greatest job when it came to spending money on players who could contribute to goal prevention.

The results of these regression analyses are pretty astonishing. The Pythagorean Win Expectation model tells us that teams need to score and prevent goals to win. I explained earlier that Ryder plotted data from 1946 to 2003 to determine the strength of the relationship between Win Expectation and actual win numbers. When he did so, he discovered that the relationship had an R-squared value of 0.935. That's a high number, indicating a strong relationship between Pythagoras' estimates, which use goals for and against, and actual wins. Yet even in the face of such clear evidence, it doesn't seem like the NHL teams of the 2003–04 season spent money on the things that helped them win games: goal scoring and prevention. Such practices ring of poor management.

So, how did team management fare in the most recent NHL season, 2008–09? Here are the two graphs representing that information:

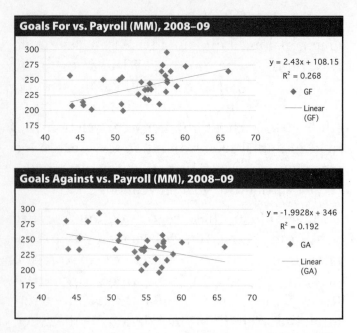

Looking at these two graphs, something might jump out at you. The scatter plots appear less random, with trends more apparent. The R-squared values agree with this assessment. The Goals For graph has an R-squared value of 0.268 (rho=0.52), far higher than 2003–04. This indicates a stronger relationship between payroll and goals for, meaning that in 2008–09 as teams spent more money they scored more goals. A similar change in the strength of the relationship between goals against and payroll occurs in the Goals Against graph, where the R-squared value rises to 0.192, up from 0.064 in 2003–04. We can see that, according to the model, higher payrolls are associated with lower goals against. It seems that something might have happened between 2003–04 and 2008–09 that pushed NHL management to allocate more resources—whether directly or indirectly—to goal scoring and prevention.

The Efficiency Cap

That "something" was, quite possibly, the 2004–05 NHL lockout. One of the major points of contention between the National Hockey League Players Association (NHLPA) and the league itself was the proposed salary cap. Players hated the idea because the cap would inevitably keep salaries down. Owners loved it for the same reason. In the end the two parties came to an agreement on a $39-million-dollar team cap that would grow annually in relation to league-wide revenues. The agreement also included a salary floor, which was set at $16 million below the cap.

Prior to the lockout and resultant salary cap, there were a variety of strategies used by NHL team management in their attempts to win hockey games. The savvy teams did as much research as possible, sought out the best available players and spent money according to their teams' revenues. Think of teams like Detroit (big market) or Carolina (small market). Another strategy was to spend money like crazy and hope it paid off. This tactic was used by teams like Dallas, who took advantage of it somewhat successfully, or by Toronto and the New York Rangers, who did not. Teams in this category didn't have to worry about spending efficiency, because if a $10-million player contract didn't pan out, these teams had plenty of resources to plug the hole as necessary. The last strategy teams used was to under-spend and hope to overachieve. Florida and Nashville are good examples of this.

The salary cap essentially eliminated the viability of two of the strategies just described. Big-market spenders no longer found solace in their deep bank accounts. Under a salary-cap regime, if a big contract didn't turn out as planned, it affected a team's ability to spend on other players, regardless of the amount of cash the team had. The cap forced big spenders to distribute their money more wisely.

The salary floor had a similar effect on teams that used the third strategy of under-spending with the hope of overachieving. The floor established a minimum amount teams were allowed to spend on their payroll. Teams below this threshold prior to the lockout had to get their payrolls up to the established minimum. When someone dictates that you have to spend more money on something, you're likely going to spend that money on something important. After all, a team's existing meager spending habits indicate frugality, so suddenly spending money on unimportant things seems irrational. If you have to spend it, spend it well. Hence, spending efficiency should increase thanks to the salary floor.

Well, that's what the *theory* says, but what does the *data* tell us? Honestly, it's probably too early to tell. But here are the Goals For vs. Payroll and Goals Against vs. Payroll graphs for the combined five seasons prior to the lockout:

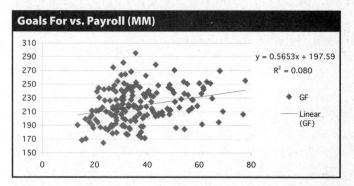

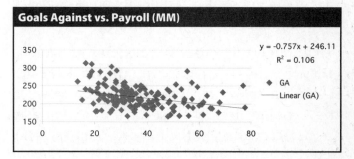

The data points in the graph represent all teams between 1998 and 2003. The relationship between goals for/against and payroll bottomed out during the 2003–04 season, perhaps adding fuel to the collective bargaining fire and the need for a salary cap. But even over the five years shown in the previous graphs, the relationship between the variables is weak. Between 1998 and 2003 the relationship between goals for and payroll had an R-squared of only 0.080. For goals against and payroll, that value was only 0.106. Contrast that with the stronger relationship we see in 2008–09 (0.268, 0.192) and the theory that the salary cap has induced teams to spend money more wisely *might* have some traction.

It's possible that after the lockout it took teams a few years to adjust to "the new NHL" as well as get team payrolls in tune with the salary cap, and from this point forward we'll see strengthening ties between payroll and the factors that win hockey games. It's also possible that 2008–09 is the product of chance. I'd bet if you asked Gary Bettman, he'd tell you it's the former.

Although there may have been some forced efficiency improvements after the implementation of the salary cap, the relationship between the variables in *any* season isn't particularly strong. Regardless of the importance of scoring and preventing goals, teams, in general, don't seem to spend their money trying to do this. This means that there are likely some teams that do it right—that is, spend money wisely—while others continue to blindly grope around, hoping to luck out and stumble on a winning strategy. We should be able to determine, objectively, which teams spend wisely, and which do not.

Marginal Payroll, Marginal Wins

Once again, we'll turn to the world of baseball analysis for an appropriate tool to solve the problem. The late Doug Pappas was a part-time lawyer, part-time sabermetrician and full-time baseball fan. Pappas was considered an expert on the business of baseball. Before his passing in 2004, Pappas wrote a recurring article for *Baseball Prospectus* entitled "Marginal Payroll, Marginal Wins."

The idea behind "Marginal Payroll, Marginal Wins" was to determine which baseball teams were the most efficient spenders. The analysis worked as follows: establish marginal benchmarks, one for wins and the other for payroll, then determine how well teams fared in relation to these standards. In Pappas' work, marginal payroll was determined by the size of a Major League Baseball roster multiplied by the league's minimum salary. Marginal Payroll represented the bare minimum a baseball team owner could spend on the team's payroll.

The other half of the equation is Marginal Wins. Essentially, this is an estimate of how many games a team would win if said team had the lowest possible payroll. Instinct might tell you that a team with the lowest possible payroll wouldn't win any games, but this isn't true. There are plenty of amateur and semi-professional baseball players who would love to jump into the major leagues at the minimum salary. A team of these players wouldn't lose every game. It helps to think about the Pythagorean Win Expectation model here, which estimates how many games a team will win based on goals for and goals against (in Pappas' analysis, runs for and runs against). Hence, a team of amateur-level players is going to score some runs but also give up some runs, and the formula tells us that luck alone will provide them with a few wins. Therefore, the Marginal Wins threshold is low, but it isn't zero.

Once the Marginal Payroll and Marginal Wins benchmarks are established, a comparison is drawn between these points of reference and the teams' actual records and payrolls. The results tell us how many wins a baseball team achieved above and beyond a team of, say, amateur players, as well as how much money the teams spent to get those extra wins. The idea is that smart teams should get more wins from less money.

It is interesting to adapt Pappas' work to the NHL, looking at the 2003–04 and 2008–09 seasons.

Perhaps then we can draw some conclusions as to which teams spend money most efficiently.

Doing it Hockey Style

The first thing we have to figure out is what constitutes a marginal hockey team, as well as how much that sort of team earns in salary. There are no specific rules to determine the marginal yardstick against which we'll measure the NHL teams. However, it makes sense that a 2003–04 marginal team will be worse than a marginal team from 2008–09. In the early season, the lowest payroll possible is the roster size multiplied by the minimum wage of the NHL, since there was no salary floor dictating how little NHL teams could spend. In the latest season, the lowest payroll is set out by the collective bargaining agreement between the NHL and the NHLPA, and it is higher than the roster size multiplied by the minimum wage. It's safe to assume that the lower possible payroll from '04 will result in a worse marginal team than one from '09. Think about it: in 2003–04 you could recruit a whole team of players making the minimum wage. But with a salary floor, like the one in 2008–09, you might fill 22 of 23 roster spots with marginal players earning the minimum wage. That last roster spot, however, has to pay enough to reach the floor. You could make an irrational decision and spend the remaining dollars by overpaying another marginally skilled player, but economics assumes people are rational. Instead, you'd spend the rest of the money on the best available player. This would make your team better. Pre- and post-salary cap are different worlds, therefore we need two different marginal benchmarks.

In 2003–04 the league's minimum wage per season was $185,000. Multiplied by the 23-man roster size, that's a total lowest-possible team payroll of only $4.25 million. If we look at the lowest actual payroll from that season, which was the Nashville Predators' $23.2 million, we see how far off that $4.25 million is from the true numbers of the NHL. Based on this, it's probably unrealistic to ice a team for four-and-a-quarter million. So let's say an owner needs to pay, at the minimum, 25 players an average of $370,000—twice the minimum salary—each (25 players because we have to account for an injury or two). That puts the total payroll at $9.25 million, which is still incredibly cheap. That'll be our marginal payroll for the 2003–04 season.

Since the marginal payroll for 2008–09 is determined by the NHL, we have the following values:

Marginal Payroll	
Season	Marginal Payroll
2003–04	$9.25 million
2008–09	$40.7 million

The next problem is figuring out just how poorly these marginal teams would perform in the NHL. For the first marginal team we can look back into recent NHL history.

Three of the worst-ever seasons belong to expansion teams. The inaugural campaign of the Washington Capitals, back in 1970, was a doozy. The Capitals shattered records no team wants to own, managing to win only one game on the road, while losing 39. They also lost 37 games in row on their way to finishing the season 8–65–5. That's a 0.103 winning percentage. More recent exercises in hockey futility come to us via the 1992 Ottawa Senators and San Jose Sharks. In a race to the bottom that became known as the "Alexander Daigle Sweepstakes," both expansion clubs ended the season with 24 points. The Sharks edged the Senators with their 11–71–2 record (0.131 winning percentage) versus Ottawa's 10–70–4 (0.119 winning percentage).

It's hard to imagine a marginal team doing much worse than any of these losers, so we will use their season standings as a guide. Let's assume that for the 2003–04 season in the analysis, a marginal team earning a marginal payroll wins 8 games in an 82-game schedule; that's a winning percentage of 0.098.

The strategy for establishing the marginal wins for the 2008–09 season is a little different. The latest season has a league-mandated minimum payroll. This minimum is far higher than the smallest amount spent in 2003–04. In the '04 season, the Detroit Red Wings had the highest payroll, paying $77.8 million to their players, while Nashville paid out only $23.2 million, the lowest in the NHL. The ratio between those payrolls is 3.4. In other words, the wealthiest teams more than tripled the payrolls of the teams with the least money. In 2008–09, the ratio between the highest and lowest payroll was only 1.5, thanks to a league-mandated minimum and maximum. Because the marginal payroll is so high in relation to the maximum payroll under a salary cap, intuition suggests that a marginal team would perform better in relation to a high-payroll team. But how much better?

Using the results of the earlier regression analysis, we can "predict" how many goals for and goals against a team with a $40.7-million payroll (the league minimum) would get. We can then plug these predicted goals for and against into the Pythagorean Win Expectation formula and get the predicted winning percentage. This value will be used for the Marginal Wins of a team for the 2008–09 season.

It turns out that a team with a $40.7-million payroll (accounting for some error, and bad luck) would score about 191 goals and have 317 scored against them. That works out to a 0.266 winning percentage. Quite a bit better than the marginal team of 2004, which we pegged at a 0.098 winning percentage. But keep in mind the NHL's collective bargaining agreement forced teams to spend about $1.5 million per player in 2009, thanks to the salary floor. Contrast that with our marginal team players from 2003–04, who only earn about $370,000 each. More money should mean better players and a better performance. Here's the summary of the benchmarks we'll use for the analysis:

Marginal Benchmarks				
Season	High Payroll	Low Payroll	Marg. Payroll	Marg. Win %
2003–04	$77.8 million	$23.2 million	$9.25 million	0.098
2008–09	$66.1 million	$43.6 million	$40.7 million	0.266

Now it's time to use our marginal teams to see how good the real teams are at spending money on players. We achieve the marginal payroll/marginal wins (MP/MW) value using the following formula:

MP/MW = (Actual Payroll – Marginal Payroll) /
(Actual Wins – Marginal Win %)

Here's an example from 2003–04:

The New York Islanders had a team payroll of $43.8 million, which means they spent $34.6 million dollars more than what we assume a marginal team would have to spend. What did they get for that $34.6 million? Well, the Islanders had a winning percentage of 0.463 in 2003–04. That's 0.365 higher than what we assume a marginal team would achieve. That 0.365 equates to about 30 wins over the course of an 82-game season. So New York spent $34.6 million more than a marginal team would spend, and got 30 more wins out of the deal. Their MP/MW value is, thus, $961,153. In order to determine if this figure is good or bad we need to compare the Islanders to another team. Let's look at the 2003–04 Montréal Canadiens.

The Canadiens had a payroll of $42.7 million, very close to New York's. However, the Habs managed to win games at a 0.500 clip. Therefore, they outperformed the 2003–04 marginal team by 0.402 (0.500 – 0.098), or about 33 wins (0.402 * 82, the number of games in a season). Montréal's MP/MW value is $840,311. What does this mean? Well, we can say that Montréal spent their payroll money more efficiently than New York did. It only cost the Canadiens $840,311 for each win beyond what a marginal team would win, while it cost the Islanders $961,153.

The calculation for the 2008–09 season is nearly identical. Simply substitute our marginal benchmarks for 2008–09 in place of the figures for 2003–04 (since, as explained, the marginal teams are different) and you're all set.

MP/MW gives us a dollar figure that can best be described as the amount of money spent on each win beyond what a marginal team (earning the marginal payroll) could manage to win. Logic dictates that smarter management will be able to earn wins more cheaply than poor management can, thus the cost of the better management's marginal wins should be cheaper. Teams will fall into one of four categories. A high MP/MW with a good record represents a team that spends a lot of money to win games, but does it successfully. These teams essentially buy championships. A high MP/MW value with a poor record indicates a badly run team, spending a lot of money for nothing. A low MP/MW number with a good record means the team is well run, spends money efficiently and finds bargains. A low MP/MW combined with a bad record means the club probably isn't spending enough money to compete with the rest of the league. These are the teams hoping to overachieve. We'll explore the data in this context.

MP/MW 2003–04				
Team	Payroll	Win %	Marg. Wins	MP/MW
ANA	54.4	0.354	21	$1,879,412
ATL	27.2	0.402	25	$488,704
BOS	45.8	0.500	33	$934,353
BUF	33.0	0.451	29	$621,461
CAR	37.8	0.341	20	$1,142,056
CGY	35.2	0.512	34	$594,747
CHI	31.6	0.244	12	$1,387,496
CLB	32.1	0.305	17	$1,008,017
COL	60.9	0.488	32	$1,435,990
DAL	67.6	0.500	33	$1,595,680
DET	77.8	0.585	40	$1,571,414
EDM	30.8	0.439	28	$565,012
FLA	26.4	0.341	20	$571,028
LAK	46.1	0.341	20	$1,557,804
MIN	26.8	0.366	22	$537,243
MTL	42.7	0.500	33	$840,311
NAS	23.2	0.463	30	$273,662
NJD	48.1	0.524	35	$946,688
NYI	43.8	0.463	30	$961,153
NYR	77.0	0.329	19	$3,269,352
OTT	39.6	0.524	35	$703,581
PHI	65.1	0.488	32	$1,567,388
PHX	37.8	0.268	14	$1,632,770
PIT	26.6	0.280	15	$775,194

MP/MW 2003–04 cont.				
Team	Payroll	Win %	Marg. Wins	MP/MW
SJS	34.8	0.524	35	$566,297
STL	61.2	0.476	31	$1,492,055
TBL	33.5	0.561	38	$487,304
TOR	61.8	0.549	37	$1,266,097
VAN	38.7	0.524	35	$677,840
WAS	51.1	0.280	15	$2,412,457

High MP/MW, Good Record

Dallas Stars, Detroit Red Wings, Philadelphia Flyers, Toronto Maple Leafs

High MP/MW, Poor Record

Washington Capitals, Phoenix Coyotes, New York Rangers, Anaheim Ducks

Low MP/MW, Good Record

Tampa Bay Lightning, San Jose Sharks, Vancouver Canucks, Calgary Flames

Low MP/MW, Poor Record

Florida Panthers, Pittsburgh Penguins, Minnesota Wild, Atlanta Thrashers

MP/MW 2008–09				
Team	Payroll	Win %	Marg. Wins	MP/MW
ANA	57.5	0.512	20	$832,871
ATL	43.5	0.427	13	$219,214

MP/MW 2008–09 cont.				
Team	Payroll	Win %	Marg. Wins	MP/MW
BOS	56.8	0.646	31	$517,571
BUF	50.6	0.500	19	$517,250
CAR	51.0	0.561	24	$428,766
CGY	58.8	0.549	23	$783,207
CHI	57.9	0.561	24	$714,941
CLB	51.2	0.390	10	$1,031,115
COL	53.4	0.500	19	$662,497
DAL	57.3	0.439	14	$1,172,752
DET	57.4	0.622	29	$573,386
EDM	55.2	0.463	16	$896,219
FLA	54.7	0.500	19	$732,124
LAK	43.8	0.415	12	$262,471
MIN	54.3	0.488	18	$751,375
MTL	57.5	0.500	19	$875,964
NAS	45.4	0.488	18	$260,446
NJD	55.0	0.622	29	$490,407
NYI	46.7	0.317	4	$1,433,859
NYR	56.3	0.524	21	$740,513
OTT	54.8	0.439	14	$998,661
PHI	66.1	0.537	22	$1,147,467
PHX	45.5	0.439	14	$339,794
PIT	56.6	0.549	23	$689,063
SJS	57.2	0.646	31	$530,428
STL	54.3	0.500	19	$711,330
TBL	50.9	0.293	2	$4,695,155
TOR	48.3	0.415	12	$626,682
VAN	53.8	0.549	23	$567,017
WAS	60.1	0.610	28	$689,904

High MP/MW, Good Record

Philadelphia Flyers, Anaheim Ducks, Calgary Flames, Chicago Blackhawks

High MP/MW, Poor Record

Tampa Bay Lightning, New York Islanders, Columbus Blue Jackets, Dallas Stars

Low MP/MW, Good Record

Boston Bruins, New Jersey Devils, Carolina Hurricanes, San Jose Sharks

Low MP/MW, Poor Record

Atlanta Thrashers, Los Angeles Kings, Phoenix Coyotes, Nashville Predators

Are there any trends between the latest season and 2003–04, the last season before the implementation of the salary cap? Philadelphia shows up as a big-spending, big-winning team both pre- and post-salary cap, which, I guess, is how GM Bobby Clarke has managed to keep his job. Tampa Bay was an efficient team in 2003–04, capturing a Stanley Cup, but by 2008–09 was an overpaid, underachieving mess. The San Jose Sharks' management displayed an ability to get value for their dollar, showing up as a low MP/MW, good-record team in both samples. The Atlanta Thrashers, on the other hand, appear unwilling to spend the money necessary to put the team over the edge. This despite having some phenomenal players, like Dany Heatley and Ilya Kovalchuk, come through their system.

For the average fan, a team's record is the best measure of how good or bad it is. But we can't forget that, at their core, NHL teams are businesses. Money and payroll provide another dimension with which to compare and judge teams. Success, therefore, can be measured by both wins and dollars. Marginal Payroll/Marginal Wins provides us with a tool to put a team's ability to win, as well as spend money, into the proper context.

Chapter Six

Gretzky's 92—Best Ever?

It didn't take Gretzky long to make a splash in the NHL. In his rookie year, 1979–80, Gretzky tied Marcel Dionne with 137 points, losing the Art Ross Trophy in a tiebreaker that was determined by total goals scored that season. The next year Gretzky won his first of seven consecutive scoring titles, potting 55 goals and 109 assists as a 20-year-old sophomore. The world was just getting a glimpse of how good Gretzky was going to turn out.

The Greatest of the Great One

The 1981–82 season saw Gretzky shred the goal-scoring record books. He was only the third NHL player to score 50 goals in 50 games, getting his 50th goal less than halfway through the season, in game number 39. On February 24, 1982, with more than a month of hockey left to play,

Gretzky scored his 76th goal of the season, tying Phil Esposito's record. Gretzky ended the season with an astonishing 92 goals, proving just how much skill separated him from second best.

In absolute terms, Gretzky's third season displayed goal-scoring ability unlike anything hockey fans had seen before, or have seen since. But was it really the best goal-scoring performance of all time? Let's see if we can determine the answer to that question with the help of statistical tools.

Absolutely Relative

Before we dive into the data we need to discuss absolute versus relative numbers. When comparing statistics like, say, a player's season goal total, it's easy to look at Alexander Ovechkin's goals this year versus Evgeni Malkin's last year. Not much has changed in the game of hockey between this season and last. But when we start to talk about "all time," things can get a bit messy. Professional hockey is an old sport, and a lot has changed over its near 100-year existence—from the quality of equipment to the rules of the game. Sometimes simply comparing numbers doesn't work when looking at players from completely different eras. Hockey isn't the only sport to face this problem. Baseball is even older and provides us with many examples of why comparing absolute numbers can cause problems.

Cy Young is probably the most well-known pitcher in baseball history. His name is even attached to the award given annually to the best pitcher in each league. Young's career spanned 22 seasons, from 1890 to 1911. His best season was probably 1901, when he went 33–10 with a 1.62 Earned Run Average (ERA). If you're at all familiar with baseball statistics, his win-loss record should sound an alarm. In modern baseball, we rarely see 20-game winners, let alone 30. Young's 33 is unheard of today. Also that same season, Young pitched 5 shutouts and 38 complete games, the latter good enough for second place in the league.

Fast-forward from 1901 to 2009. Roy Halladay pitches for the Toronto Blue Jays. He's one of today's most dominant pitchers, making five career all-star appearances and winning the American League's Cy Young Award in 2003 (he was also nominated five times). During the 2003 season in which he was the majors' best pitcher, Halladay led the league in wins, with 22. He was also at the top in games started with 36 and complete games with 9.

Suppose you are discussing these pitchers and their ability to throw complete games. What sense does it make to compare Halladay's numbers to Young's? Young threw more complete games in eight different seasons than Halladay has thrown in his entire career. Does this mean Halladay is inferior at throwing complete games? Of course not. He led the league in 2003, and he's the best for that particular statistic. The problem is that the eras are not directly comparable, thus comparing the players' absolute numbers can cause problems. What matters is that, relative to players of their generation, both Young and Halladay are extremely proficient pitchers.

The point is that a player's statistics need to be discussed in the context of his time and place. Hockey's problems are not as pronounced as baseball's since the game hasn't changed quite as drastically, but they exist nonetheless. We need look no further than absolute goal numbers. Gretzky's 92-goal season is impressive, there's no doubt about that. But do you really think Maurice Richard had a crack at that record, playing only 50 or 60 games per season? What about Jarome Iginla during the trap-stifled years at the start of the new millennium? The fact of the matter is, goal totals depend on the amount of offense in the league, and that offense has fluctuated greatly over the course of professional hockey history. Here's a graph of league-wide goals per game, from 1954 to 2008:

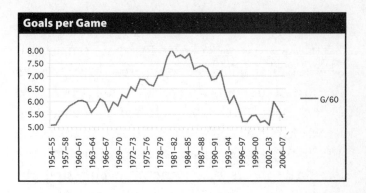

Goals per Game

The league-goals-per-game graph peaks precisely at the 1981–82 season. That just happens to be the year Gretzky broke the single-season goal-scoring record. During that period, goals were easier to score, relative to other years. Therefore, to determine whether or not his was the greatest goal-scoring season of all time we need to account for the huge offensive output across the league. One method of doing so is to compare a player to his peers' performances during the same season. The idea is that it's not how much you score, but how much more you score than the next best guy. It's better to get 50 goals in a world where the next best is 10, than score 100 in a world where the average is 90—relatives, not absolutes.

Fishin' with Statistics

Thanks to the work of Alan Ryder, we can develop a game plan that'll help to compare a player's results to those of his compatriots. In a 2004 paper titled "The Poisson Toolbox," published on his website, Ryder demonstrated that goal scoring in hockey is a Poisson process. In statistics, a Poisson process is a series of discrete, random events that are described by a specific probability distribution. Essentially, a Poisson process has a predictable relationship between a specific event and the average of other events over some interval. That may sound a bit heavy, but it's a really simple concept. Let's say your personal golf scores follow a Poisson probability distribution. You've played 10 rounds of golf this year, with the following scores: 88, 91, 90, 91, 81, 85, 87, 87, 90 and 94. The average of those 10 rounds is 88. What is the probability that your next round will be lower than, say, 85? We can use the Poisson function to figure this out. That function is:

$$P(85) = (88^{85} * e^{-85}) / 88!$$

Pretty intense. Fortunately, most spreadsheet software has this function built in, so finding the answer involves little more than entering the average (88) and the score you're looking for (85). It turns out that the probability of you achieving a score of 85 or better on your next round of golf is about 40 percent.

Going back to Gretzky, outside of building a time machine, traveling back to 1981, kidnapping him and holding him ransom *Misery*-style, there's no way to determine how that year would turn out sans Gretzky, right? Well, with Ryder's insight that hockey goal scoring is a Poisson process, or in his words "Poisson enough," we can simulate, using statistical methods, the outcome of that season as if Gretzky wasn't there at all. Doing so will tell us, based on the level of competition, just how good his 1981–82 season really was.

The idea is to determine the probability of someone else scoring 92 goals that season. The less likely this possibility, the more spectacular—and rare—Gretzky's performance was that year. At the end of the 1981–82 campaign, Mike Bossy finished second to Gretzky's 92 goals with 64. What are the odds of Bossy scoring as many goals as The Great One if we could repeat the season? Using the Poisson formula, Bossy has a 0.039 percent chance of scoring 92 goals if everything was done again. The number 0.039 might sound a bit odd, but what it implies is that if the 1981–82 season was played over, and over, and over, Bossy would score 92 (or more) goals 0.039 percent of the time.

For comparison's sake, Gretzky would score 92 goals (or more) 47 percent of the time.

But wait a minute: if we simulated the season over again, wouldn't Gretzky score exactly 92 goals? And wouldn't Bossy come out with 64, no more, no less? The answer is possibly, but unlikely. Think about your golf scores again. The average of the scores was 88, but this doesn't mean that you shot 88 every round, nor did it imply with 100 percent certainty that you will shoot 88 in your next round. The goal-scoring totals of the 1981–82 season work the same way. Consider all the randomness that occurs over the course of an NHL season, and how everything has to fall just so for it to turn out, for a second time, exactly as it did the first. If the entire season was played over again, it is highly unlikely that each play would happen identically, resulting in the exact same goal totals. Maybe Mark Messier hits a few more goal posts. Maybe Bossy breaks his stick at a crucial moment. There are far too many variables that determine the outcome of a shot, a period, a game, a series or a season for them all to fall into place in the same manner a second time around. This notion, that a small change can have huge effects on seemingly unrelated variables, is known as the Butterfly Effect.

So as we repeatedly re-enact the 1981–82 season, there exists some random chance—albeit a very slim one—that Bossy eventually scores 92 goals. That probability is determined by the Poisson function and is, as noted, 0.039 percent. Dennis Maruk, who placed third in goal scoring in 1981–82 with 60, also has some probability of scoring 92 goals in our many iterations of the campaign. But because his goal-scoring total was lower than Bossy's, Maruk's likelihood of scoring 92 goals is only 0.004 percent. With 55 goals, Dino Ciccarelli placed fourth in 1981–82 goal scoring. The Poisson function tells us he'll only score 92 goals 0.0002 percent of the time.

To find the total probability of someone having a season as good as Gretzky's in 1981–82, we have to calculate the chance each player had that year of scoring 92 goals. It turns out that these probabilities go to zero pretty quickly. That makes sense intuitively; as players score less and less, it is more and more difficult for them to have any chance of reaching 92, even through pure luck. If we could play the season over again, a player who scored 7 goals in 1981–82 needs an awful lot of luck to get to 92. So much luck, in fact, we may as well call it impossible. So, for our purposes, we'll only look at the top 20 goal scorers behind Gretzky that season—his goal-scoring "peers." Here's the list, along with how many goals each player scored and their chance of breaking Gretzky's record if the season was repeated:

Players' Chances at 92 in 1981–82		
Player	G	Probability
Mike Bossy	64	0.000393608116348
Dennis Maruk	60	0.000047458360678
Dino Ciccarelli	55	0.000001897161469
Rick Vaive	54	0.000000913989680
Blaine Stoughton	52	0.000000192830638
Rick Middleton	51	0.000000084230861
Marcel Dionne	50	0.000000035516491
Mark Messier	50	0.000000035516491
Bryan Trottier	50	0.000000035516491
Peter Stastny	46	0.000000000764888
Bill Barber	45	0.000000000263926
Dale Hawerchuk	45	0.000000000263926
Al Secord	44	0.000000000087010
Barry Pederson	44	0.000000000087010
Brian Propp	44	0.000000000087010
Morris Lukowich	43	0.000000000027324
Bobby Smith	43	0.000000000027324
Michel Goulet	42	0.000000000008159
Mark Napier	40	0.000000000000605
Lanny McDonald	40	0.000000000000605

The sum of those tiny numbers is 0.00044426, or approximately 0.044 percent.

So what does that mean, and how does it tell us how good Gretzky's 92-goal season was? Well, the Poisson process says that if we were able to somehow play the 1981–82 season over and over again, without Gretzky, one of the players in the previous list would break his record, on average, once every 2250 seasons. But is that rare? To find out, we can calculate the same thing for other seasons known for their great goal-scoring performances. The more unlikely—the lower the probability—that the 20 next best scorers would break the goal leader's total, the greater the individual performance of that leader. Let's take a peek.

Gordie Howe, 49 goals, 1952–53

Mr. Hockey's highest-scoring season was over half a century ago. Howe potted 49 goals and 46 assists in 70 games played. The runner-up was teammate Ted Lindsay with 30 goals. Maurice Richard scored 28 goals that year, good for fourth spot. So how good was Howe's season? It would take the rest of the league of 1952–53 about 400 seasons to produce another 49-goal scorer.

Maurice Richard, 50 goals, 1944–45

The first player to score 50 goals in 50 games, the Rocket outdistanced second-place Herb Cain by

18 goals. In order for someone to break Richard's record, the six-team league would have to play 670 iterations of the season.

Phil Esposito, 76 goals, 1970–71

This is the season with the highest goal total before Gretzky broke the record. Esposito had a tremendous year, scoring 25 more goals than second-place John Bucyk and 32 more than third-place Bobby Hull. The odds of somebody in the 1970–71 top 20 breaking this record if we repeated the season? About 1 in 2400, which actually makes Esposito's season more exceptional than Gretzky's 92-goal campaign.

Mario Lemieux, 85 goals, 1988–89

Mario the Magnificent was certainly a force, but his top goal-scoring season doesn't match up with the best. In fact, 1 in 24 replays of the 1988–89 season would produce an 85-goal scorer.

Brett Hull, 86 goals, 1990–91

An unbelievable performance by the Golden Brett. Hull outpaced his nearest competitors—Cam Neely, Steve Yzerman and Theo Fleury—by 35 goals.

You'd need to repeat the 1990–91 season about 105,000 times before seeing someone else from that season score as many goals as Hull did. That's extremely rare, much more so than Gretzky's 1981-82 season.

One possible caveat: because of an injury that prevented him from completing the entire season, goal-scoring runner-up Cam Neely managed only 51 goals in just 69 games played. Neely surely would have added a few more goals had he been able to play more games—goals that would have made Hull's performance less rare. Yet, even if we adjust the results based on goals per 80 games, giving Neely 59 goals (and Hull 88), the odds of someone in the top 20 of that season beating Hull are still 1 in 55,000.

Wayne Gretzky, 87 goals, 1983–84

Two years after his record-breaking 92-goal season, Gretzky netted 87 goals, good for the second highest yearly goal-scoring total ever. Amazingly, this performance was even more tremendous than Gretzky's record-breaking season. The Great One finished 31 goals ahead of second-place Michel Goulet, and was 33 better than third- and fourth-place Tim Kerr and

Glenn Anderson. The odds of an 87-goal 1983–84 season without Gretzky? About 1 in 12,000.

Goal Probability Results			
Player	Year	G	Probability
Brett Hull	1990–91	86	1 in 105000
Wayne Gretzky	1983–84	87	1 in 12000
Phil Esposito	1970–71	76	1 in 2400
Wayne Gretzky	1981–82	92	1 in 2250
Maurice Richard	1944–45	50	1 in 670
Gordie Howe	1952–53	49	1 in 400
Mario Lemieux	1988–89	85	1 in 24

According to the above analysis, Gretzky's record-breaking 92-goal season was not the best goal-scoring performance ever. That honor goes to Brett Hull in 1990–91. As a matter of fact, the 92-goal season wasn't even Gretzky's best; he was better in 1983–84. These results demonstrate the value of looking at relative rather than absolute performances. Hull and Lemieux had near-identical goal totals in the two seasons examined here, but Hull's performance outshines Lemieux's because 1988–89 saw higher goal totals across the league than what was observed in 1990–91. When goals are abundant, high goal totals are usually less exceptional.

Despite these results, it's unlikely Gretzky's 92-goal performance will be topped any time soon.

The biggest threat likely comes from Washington's Alexander Ovechkin. Ovechkin's highest goal total so far was in 2007–08, when he scored 65. How many times would we have to repeat that season before Ovie scored 92 goals or more? About 16,000 times.

Chapter Seven

Ryder's Player Contribution

Whether it's giving a movie two thumbs-up, getting a B+ on an English paper or rating a Mexican resort with five stars, our culture is obsessed with expressing the quality of something in a succinct, easy-to-understand manner. Doing so makes comparing subjects easy; a B+ beats a B−, five stars beats four and two thumbs-up is better than none at all. In the hockey world, though, things aren't quite so straightforward. We do have simple measurements—goals, assists, penalty minutes—but there is no easy way to answer the question, "Is player A better than player B?"

Comparison among hockey players is even more difficult when we start looking across positions. It's easy to say that Buffalo's Thomas Vanek is better than his teammate Clarke MacArthur; for a quick evaluation we need only look at the two forwards' goal totals. But are Vanek and his 40 goals better, or more valuable, than Chicago Blackhawks defenseman Brent Seabrook? And how do these players compare in value to, say, Anaheim's young netminder Jonas Hiller? These are difficult questions to answer, especially objectively, but the answers are extremely important to NHL management. Teams need to fill out their rosters with forwards, defensemen and goaltenders. Without knowing the relative value of each player, efficient roster allocation is nearly impossible. So, management is forced to guess.

For this reason, the idea of a single metric that represents the value of a player is an appealing prospect. With this sort of knowledge, establishing an NHL lineup would be nothing more than a mathematical exercise. While this concept might irk some hockey purists, the idea is certainly exciting to the business people running NHL franchises, as well as to hockey analysts. But before a person can run, he must learn to walk. As the data collection and publication of NHL statistics improved, Alan Ryder decided to take the first steps.

Contributing to the Game of Hockey

Ryder defines his Player Contribution system as "a method for allocating credit for a team's performance to the individual contributors on a hockey team." The system is a wonderfully complex series of calculations that seeks to divide among the players the credit for a team's wins. The beauty of Player Contribution (PC) is its leveling of the positional playing field; in the words of the author, "It puts offense, defense and goaltending performance on the same page, in the same currency." Ryder published his PC methodology in a paper on his website, hockeyanalytics.com, in 2003.[1]

The foundation of PC is the idea of Marginal Goals. "Marginal" means exactly what you think: something "on the border," the lower bound. In the world of professional hockey, having "zero" as a minimum benchmark—the lower bound—makes little sense. A "marginal" forward isn't someone like your grandmother, who would probably play terrible defense and score zero goals and zero assists if she was on the ice. The NHL is composed of the best players in the world, and a player who performed as poorly as your grandmother could (and would) be easily replaced by someone better, perhaps from junior hockey or a semi-pro league. Therefore, the marginal player isn't the one with

---

1. To get the best understanding of the PC system, I urge you to read the original paper. Spanning 80 pages, it may seem somewhat daunting to the analytical layman, but Ryder is an adept writer as well as a pioneer in the field. From the horse's mouth, as they say.

the worst possible statistics. Instead, a marginal player can be thought of as a person whose ability is equal to that of the best player who is *not* in the NHL. The marginal player is much better than "zero."

In the same vein, Marginal Goals represents the goal production (and prevention) of a marginal team. This team isn't made up of random people from the earth's population, but consists of actual hockey players. Consider a marginal team as a sort of semi-pro all-star team. A team like this wouldn't score zero goals in the NHL, if given the opportunity, and since this is the most realistic version of "the worst," it makes no sense to compare the performances of actual NHL teams against the extreme minimum of "zero." Instead, they should be compared to the performance of such a fictional team—the marginal team.

Marginal Goals, then, is the number of goals an NHL team has scored above the total of the hypothetical marginal team. But since Player Contribution is concerned with defense, too, Marginal Goals also accounts for the amount of goals an NHL team prevents beyond the total of those prevented by the marginal team. Perhaps an example is in order:

In 2008–09, the NHL average goals for and against was 239. Ryder's methodology assigns

58 percent of the game to defense, and thus a marginal team would score 58 percent of 239 goals—139. This marginal team would also allow 158 percent of 239 goals—378. In 2008–09, the Los Angeles Kings scored 207 goals and had 234 goals scored against. To calculate Marginal Goals, we need to find the difference between the actual and marginal team. The Kings outperformed the marginal offense by 68 goals and the marginal defense by 144 goals. That gives Los Angeles a total of 212 Marginal Goals. Looking at another team, the Vancouver Canucks buried 246 goals and allowed 220. Vancouver scored 107 more goals than the marginal team and allowed 158 fewer, for a total of 265 Marginal Goals.

Ryder defines a marginal team in such a way that it will win zero games, even though it will score some goals. By scoring or preventing goals beyond this minimum standard, an NHL team will begin to win games. The better a team outperforms this standard, the more games that team will win. In the example of the Canucks, we expect Vancouver to have a better record than Los Angeles because the Canucks' Marginal Goal total is much higher than the Kings'. In fact, Vancouver finished the 2008–09 season with a record of 45–27–10. Los Angeles finished 34–37–11. With Marginal Goals in hand, we have a way of seeing how and why an NHL team gets its actual record: by outscoring and preventing more goals than a hypothetical marginal team. The next step is to figure out how to distribute these Marginal Goals to the players.

At this point, the methodology of Ryder's paper exceeds the scope of this book. He divides Marginal Goals into scoring and prevention, isolates defense and enumerates goaltending; he makes adjustments for situations—power plays, short-handedness or even-strength. He also transforms the results into easily manageable numbers then hands out bite-sized chunks to each player according to merit. But what we're concerned about here is the end result; after 80 pages and 25,000 words, Ryder's Player Contribution provides us with a single number with which to compare players of any make, style or position.

Here are the top 10 skaters and goaltenders from the 2002–03 season, according to the PC system:

Top Skaters			
Player	Team	Position	PC
Nicklas Lidstrom	DET	D	124
Al MacInnis	STL	D	114
Markus Naslund	VAN	LW	110
Milan Hejduk	COL	RW	109
Sergei Zubov	DAL	D	106
Sergei Gonchar	WAS	D	103
Scott Niedermayer	NJD	D	99

Top Skaters cont.

Player	Team	Position	PC
Dany Heatley	ATL	RW	98
Marian Hossa	OTT	RW	98
Dan Boyle	TBL	D	98

Top Goalies

Player	Team	PC
Roberto Luongo	FLA	243
Marty Turco	DAL	183
Ed Belfour	TOR	178
Olaf Kolzig	WAS	175
Jean-Sebastien Giguere	ANA	175
Patrick Roy	COL	172
Mike Dunham	NYR	164
Dwayne Roloson	MIN	154
Tomas Vokoun	NAS	144
Roman Cechmanek	PHI	142

I separated the top players into two tables to prevent the list from being dominated by a single position. In fact, the top 12 PC point-getters are goaltenders. And to be honest, I'm not exactly sure what to think of that. Perhaps Ryder's system puts too much emphasis on defense, thus over-valuing goaltenders relative to other players. The results could also mean that good goalies are an extremely valuable piece of the team puzzle. I'm choosing to believe the latter, because I've seen what a hot goaltender can do over a small sample of games, like an NHL playoff series. I think a goalie has more opportunity than any other player to impact game outcomes, and thus great goalies will end up influencing many more games over the course of a season than, say, a right-winger, resulting in a major accumulation of PC points for goalies.

The exciting thing about these two lists is how the players are ranked and rated. Rather than trying to determine the relative positions of the players by examining a multitude of statistics, Player Contribution takes all the dimensions of a player's performance into account and puts them together to result in an easy-to-understand single number—just how we like it. Let's examine the numbers in detail. The 2002–03 goalie rankings are fairly close from spots 2 through 10. Way out in front of the group is Roberto Luongo, besting second-place Marty Turco by 60 points. Player Contribution tells us just how important Luongo was to the Florida Panthers that year.

Of the top 10 skaters, six are defensemen. More specifically, they're offensive defensemen. Since Ryder's system likes both offense and defense, players that excel in these two areas get a lot of credit. Nicklas Lidstrom's an absolute stud, probably one of the best defensemen of all time, and he has the PC points to back it up. Outside of Scott Niedermayer, the defensemen on the list make up the top five point scorers at the position. Niedermayer is only the 22nd highest-scoring defenseman, but manages to make our list on the back of strong defensive play.

The first two forwards in the table, Markus Naslund and Milan Hejduk, finished second and fourth in the league's scoring race. The 2002–03 Art Ross Trophy winner, Peter Forsberg, doesn't show up until the 12th position in Player Contribution, obviously outside of the top 10. Part of Ryder's methodology includes a Goals Created formula that gives more PC credit to goals than assists. Although Forsberg led the league that year with 106 points, he only scored 29 goals. Naslund scored 48 to go with his 56 assists, and Hejduk led the NHL in goals with 50.

One of the greatest things about Player Contribution, though, is how it breaks down into specific situational components. Let's look at these two players from 2002–03:

Player Contribution: Datsyuk vs. Kovalev					
Player	Team	Position	PC	PCO	PCD
Pavel Datsyuk	DET	C	52	37.5	14.5
Alexei Kovalev	PIT	RW	52	54.8	-2.9

Both Pavel Datsyuk and Alexei Kovalev managed to accumulate 52 PC points, implying that they were equally valuable during the 2002–03 season. However, both players earned their credit from entirely different angles. In the table, PCO and PCD represent how many PC points each player earned on offense (PCO) and defense (PCD). On the strength of 37 goals and 40 assists, Kovalev is credited with 54.8 PCO points for his offense. Datsyuk managed only 51 points and therefore 37.5 PCO points for his efforts. On the other side of the ledger, Datsyuk's stellar defensive play (worth a future Selke Trophy) earned him 14.5 PCD points. Kovalev? Not so much. Player Contribution verifies what many fans have witnessed in person: Kovalev is amazing with the puck, but his laziness can make him a liability on defense. His PCD total is *negative*. That's a pretty fascinating result. It allows us to compare, on equal footing, two players with completely different on-ice personas—in this case a lackadaisical phenom and a defensive specialist.

But that's not all Ryder's system can teach us. Here are two other similar centermen:

Player Contribution: Conroy vs. Rolston						
Player	Team	PC	PCO	PCOEV	PCOPPP	PCOSH	PCOPPO
Craig Conroy	CGY	62	42.1	34.1	6.8	0.6	0.7
Brian Rolston	BOS	63	41.9	22.7	10.3	9.7	-0.9

Craig Conroy and Brian Rolston have comparable PC points, and both contributed equally in their offense (PCO). Once again, the nuances of Player Contribution allow us to see how these two players differ. PCOEV represents each player's contribution at even strength, PCOPPP is power-play production and PCOSH is for short-handed situations. And, as defined by Ryder, PCOPPO is "power play opportunities," which is a player's contribution from a penalty-drawing standpoint.

From the data we can see that Conroy contributes most of his offense at even strength, with some on the power play and very little on the penalty kill. He also shows little aptitude at drawing penalties. Rolston earned half of his PCO credits on special teams and half at even strength. Rolston also shows a less-than-average propensity to draw penalties. Here are two players with similar overall offensive contributions who arrived at those totals in different ways: Conroy as the straight second-line center and Rolston as the special-teams expert.

Ryder set out to develop a system that allowed the comparison of any player to another. His research led to Player Contribution. Now, with this powerful tool at our disposal, let's put it to the test...of conventional wisdom.

Do the Awards Voters Get it Right?

Every year the NHL hands out awards to deserving players based on their previous season's performances in a variety of categories. The responsibility of determining who gets what falls into the collective lap of the Professional Hockey Writers Association. The PHWA is a 400-member fraternity of journalists who write for a multitude of newspapers, magazines and most recently, websites. It's safe to assume that these guys watch a ton of hockey every year. One of the lessons of this book, though, is that perception and reality often conflict. How can we tell if these writers are voting for the right people? Perhaps Player Contribution can help us get to the bottom of this interesting question.

Awarded annually to the NHL's Most Valuable Player, the Hart Trophy is the "big one," the award that everybody wants to win. Player Contribution breaks down a team's wins into individual performances, so it seems like the perfect method with which to measure the actual most valuable player. Let's take a peek at what happened in three recent seasons.

The three nominees for the award from the 2005–06 season were Joe Thornton, Jaromir Jagr and Miikka Kiprusoff. Thornton led the league in points, scoring 29 goals and adding 96 assists on the strength of a breakout season by teammate

Jonathan Cheechoo. As the eventual winner, Thornton was the first person to receive the Hart Trophy after switching teams mid-season, following his move from the Boston Bruins to the San Jose Sharks in a trade. Jagr was the runner-up to Thornton in the points standings, scoring 54 goals and adding 69 assists. Kiprusoff was seen as the heart of a strong Calgary team, backstopping them to 46 wins. The Kipper finished the season with an impressive 0.923 save percentage.

If we were forced to choose the trophy winner from these players according to their PC values, we would make our selection based on results that look like this:

Player Contribution 2005–06: Hart Trophy Nominees			
Player	Team	Position	PC
Miikka Kiprusoff	CGY	G	215
Jaromir Jagr	NYR	RW	119
Joe Thornton	SJS	C	100

Kiprusoff outperforms both forwards by a large margin. But unless your name is Dominik Hasek, it's a rare event at which a goaltender wins the Hart. If we make the assumption that the PHWA is unlikely to pick a goalie for the award, the writers still got it wrong by picking Thornton over Jagr, the latter outperforming the former by nearly 20 percent.

But let's go back a step. Did the NHL even get the nominees right? Here's the list of the top 10 PC point-earners from 2005–06, excluding goalies:

Player Contribution 2005–06: Top 10			
Player	Team	Position	PC
Sergei Zubov	DAL	D	150
Nicklas Lidstrom	DET	D	143
Alexander Ovechkin	WAS	LW	137
Simon Gagne	PHI	LW	130
Chris Pronger	EDM	D	130
Brian Gionta	NJD	RW	124
Jonathan Cheechoo	SJS	RW	124
Brad Richards	TBL	C	123
Jaromir Jagr	NYR	RW	119
Henrik Zetterberg	DET	LW	113

According to Ryder's system, there were eight players more valuable than Jagr, and the actual award-winner, Thornton, doesn't even crack the top 10. Player Contribution tells us that the Dallas Stars' Sergei Zubov deserved the nod as the league's most valuable player.

In 2006–07 the NHL nominated, for the Hart, two goalies—Martin Brodeur of the New Jersey Devils and Roberto Luongo of the Vancouver Canucks—alongside the Pittsburgh Penguins' young phenom, Sidney Crosby. Following the unwritten rule that goalies rarely win MVP,

Crosby took home the trophy with 49 percent of the PHWA's votes. This despite the fact his 123 PC points were dwarfed by Brodeur's 268 and Luongo's 279. The league almost had it right with the two netminders who were nominated—they finished one-two in the league in Player Contribution—but how does Crosby stack up against his fellow skaters from the 2006–07 season?

Player Contribution 2006–07: Top 10			
Player	**Team**	**Position**	**PC**
Vincent Lecavalier	TBL	C	135
Martin St. Louis	TBL	RW	132
Marian Hossa	ATL	RW	132
Nicklas Lidstrom	DET	D	130
Pavel Datsyuk	DET	C	124
Sidney Crosby	PIT	C	123
Sergei Zubov	DAL	D	113
Jarome Iginla	CGY	RW	113
Tomas Kaberle	TOR	D	110
Teemu Selanne	ANA	RW	109

Five players, including Tampa Bay Lightning teammates Vincent Lecavalier and Martin St. Louis, were more valuable to their team than Crosby was to the Pittsburgh Penguins.

In 2007–08 Pittsburgh's Evgeni Malkin, Calgary's Jarome Iginla and Washington's Alexander

Ovechkin were named as finalists for the Hart Trophy. Player Contribution says that Ovechkin and his 162 PC points deserved the award, beating out Iginla's 141 and Malkin's 113. The PHWA agreed and gave Ovie the nod. Here are the top 10 skaters from that season:

Player Contribution 2007–08: Top 10			
Player	Team	Position	PC
Alexander Ovechkin	WAS	LW	162
Jarome Iginla	CGY	RW	141
Pavel Datsyuk	DET	C	132
Ilya Kovalchuk	ATL	LW	124
Nicklas Lidstrom	DET	D	121
Henrik Zetterberg	DET	LW	121
Joe Thornton	SJS	C	115
Evgeni Malkin	PIT	C	113
Daniel Alfredsson	OTT	RW	109
Brent Burns	MIN	D	107

Besides Malkin, who might have received a bit of credit from his good playoff run, as well as from performing well on a team that lost its star for much of the season, the league was spot-on in its nominations this year. Ovechkin and Iginla were the top two PC point-getters, excluding goaltenders, for the season.

With more hits than misses for the NHL MVP, how did the league and PHWA do for the

Norris Trophy, given annually to the NHL's best defenseman? In 2005–06 the nominees were Lidstrom, Niedermayer and Zubov. Zubov and Lidstrom finished at the top of the PC list of defensemen, with 150 and 143, respectively. Niedermayer, however, was nowhere near the top, finishing 17th in the league with 76 PC points. Lidstrom snatched the award from Zubov, but no one can argue the decision was a terrible one on the PHWA's part. And just for curiosity's sake, here are the top 10 defensemen by PC from 2005–06:

Player Contribution 2005–06: Top 10 Defensemen		
Player	Team	PC
Sergei Zubov	DAL	150
Nicklas Lidstrom	DET	143
Chris Pronger	EDM	130
Tomas Kaberle	TOR	107
Dan Boyle	TBL	101
Lubomir Visnovsky	LAK	101
Mathieu Schneider	DET	96
Tom Preissing	SJS	93
Brian Rafalski	NJD	93
Dion Phaneuf	CGY	89

The 2006–07 season saw Anaheim teammates Chris Pronger and Niedermayer nominated for the Norris Trophy, alongside Lidstrom, who was defending his title as the NHL's best defenseman. Player Contribution puts Lidstrom way out in front of the trio, with 130 PC points. Niedermayer managed 101 PC points, Pronger 96. Though Lidstrom topped them all and deservedly won his second Norris in a row, Ryder's system tells us that there were better nominees for this award than the two Ducks who were up for it. Here are the top 10 defensemen of 2006–07:

Player Contribution 2006–07: Top 10 Defensemen		
Player	Team	PC
Nicklas Lidstrom	DET	130
Sergei Zubov	DAL	113
Tomas Kaberle	TOR	110
Scott Niedermayer	ANA	101
Chris Pronger	ANA	96
Dan Boyle	TBL	94
Philippe Boucher	DAL	93
Brian Rafalski	NJD	92
Lubomir Visnovsky	LAK	92
Sami Salo	VAN	90

Lidstrom won his sixth Norris in seven years in 2007–08, a streak not seen since the days of the great Bobby Orr. Lidstrom topped the list of defensemen in PC points with 121, far ahead of fellow nominees Dion Phaneuf of the Flames and Zdeno Chara of the Bruins. Neither Chara nor

Phaneuf were terrible choices as candidates, but Player Contribution tells us there were better options. Minnesota Wild blueliner Brent Burns flew completely under the radar, earning 107 PC points, good for second place.

Player Contribution 2007–08: Top 10 Defensemen		
Player	Team	PC
Nicklas Lidstrom	DET	121
Brent Burns	MIN	107
Brian Rafalski	DET	105
Zdeno Chara	BOS	97
Mike Green	WAS	97
Dion Phaneuf	CGY	93
Tomas Kaberle	TOR	93
Adrian Aucoin	CGY	88
Andrei Markov	MTL	83
Duncan Keith	CHI	83

Lidstrom's unparalleled performances have made it pretty easy for the league writers to get the Norris Trophy winner right. The nominees, however, seem to get their spots based on a dose of ability and dash of reputation.

As we've seen, Ryder's system places a lot of value on goaltending, with goalies dominating the overall PC standings each season. Although this makes it difficult to compare skaters to goaltenders for, say, the MVP trophy, comparing goalies to goalies is a simple matter for Player Contribution. Here are the top 10 goalies from 2005–06:

Player Contribution 2005–06: Top 10 Goalies		
Player	Team	PC
Henrik Lundqvist	NYR	253
Tomas Vokoun	NAS	245
Roberto Luongo	FLA	236
Miikka Kiprusoff	CGY	215
Martin Gerber	CAR	166
Martin Brodeur	NJD	162
Manny Fernandez	MIN	158
Cristobal Huet	MTL	157
Jean-Sebastien Giguere	ANA	154
Dominik Hasek	OTT	149

The three nominees for the Vezina Trophy (for best goaltender in the league) were Brodeur, Kiprusoff and the New York Rangers' Henrik Lundqvist. Unlike the majority of the NHL awards, the league's general managers vote on the Vezina. But, different crew, same results. The GMs decided that Kiprusoff earned the award, with 215 PC points, but Lundqvist—and his league-leading 253 PC points—was the far more worthy candidate. Player Contribution also tells us that two other goaltenders not even nominated for the trophy deserved to be ahead of Kiprusoff, and that Brodeur was only the sixth best goalie in the league.

The 2006–07 season saw a tie for third place in its nominees for the Vezina, with Lundqvist and Kiprusoff neck and neck. Brodeur and Luongo were the two other goalies up for the award, and Player Contribution tells us that Luongo, with 279 PC points, deserved to win over Brodeur who stole the trophy on the shoulders of a 268 PC point performance. His PC points placed him second behind Luongo but well ahead of Lundqvist's 223 and Kiprusoff's 154. So, the PC system agrees with Luongo and Brodeur as candidates for the Vezina in 2006–07—and to a lesser extent Lundqvist—but the nominators completely missed the boat with Kiprusoff, who didn't even place in the top 10 goalies that year:

Player Contribution 2006–07: Top 10 Goalies		
Player	Team	PC
Roberto Luongo	VAN	279
Martin Brodeur	NJD	268
Kari Lehtonen	ATL	247
Rick DiPietro	NYI	242
Henrik Lundqvist	NYR	223
Jean-Sebastien Giguere	ANA	187
Tim Thomas	BOS	184
Chris Mason	NAS	180
Marc-Andre Fleury	PIT	176
Ray Emery	OTT	172

Brodeur went on to capture his second consecutive Vezina—and fourth in five years—
after the 2007–08 season. His 259 PC-point
performance was second in the league, so it's
pretty hard to argue the trophy was unde-
served. Lundqvist received a third consecutive
nomination, but only managed 189 PC points,
good for sixth place in the netminder depart-
ment. The other nominee was San Jose's
Evgeni Nabokov. The panel was way off on that
one. Nabokov played behind a great San Jose
Sharks team, on the way to a league-leading
46 wins. And we know how much people like
wins, but Player Contribution goes deeper than
this superficial rating. Nabokov played in more
games than any other goalie in 2007–08, but
he only managed to accumulate 92 PC points,
lower than 25 other goalies. Tomas Vokoun led
the league, but for the second time in three
years couldn't even snag a nomination. This is
odd considering Vokoun had terrific performances with two different teams, Nashville in
2005–06 and Florida in 2007–08. Apparently
the NHL's general managers aren't much better
at finding the "best" than a bunch of journalists. That's slightly disturbing. Here are the top
10 from 2007–08:

Player Contribution 2007–08: Top 10 Goalies		
Player	Team	PC
Tomas Vokoun	FLA	267
Martin Brodeur	NJD	259
Jean-Sebastien Giguere	ANA	232
Tim Thomas	BOS	200
Roberto Luongo	VAN	199
Henrik Lundqvist	NYR	189
Mathieu Garon	EDM	180
Manny Legace	STL	173
Ilya Bryzgalov	PHX	167
Carey Price	MTL	157

I've discussed how difficult defense is to measure numerically, so the PHWA has their hands full with the Selke Trophy, given to the league's top defensive forward. More than any other, this award is subject to opinion and reputation. But as previously demonstrated, Ryder's analysis breaks down a player's contribution into offense and defense. What looks like a difficult decision to a journalist is nothing more than some spreadsheet work for Ryder.

In 2005–06, the Selke nominees were Rod Brind'Amour of the Carolina Hurricanes, Mike Fisher of the Ottawa Senators and Jere Lehtinen of the Dallas Stars. To determine which of these guys was the best defensive forward, we'll look at their PCD points—Player Contribution Defense.

Player Contribution 2005–06: Top 10 Defensive Forwards			
Player	Team	Position	PCD
Brad Richards	TBL	C	45
Jay Pandolfo	NJD	LW	45
Jere Lehtinen	DAL	RW	43
Martin St. Louis	TBL	RW	38
Simon Gagne	PHI	LW	36
Kevyn Adams	CAR	C	33
Justin Williams	CAR	RW	32
Rod Brind'Amour	CAR	C	32
Tony Amonte	CGY	RW	31
Henrik Zetterberg	DET	LW	31

Of the three nominees, PC says that Lehtinen deserved the award. He accumulated 43 PCD points, more than half of his total Player Contribution for the season. Brind'Amour was the second best of the three, with 32 PCD points. Fisher was a distant third, with 11. Brind'Amour ended up winning the trophy, which isn't completely terrible, considering how hard it is to evaluate defense. But Fisher's nomination threatens to implode the PC algorithm. Fisher was the 159th best defensive forward according to the system. In fact, Fisher wasn't even one of the five best defensive forwards on his *team*. What do the voters see that Ryder's system doesn't?

Brind'Amour defended his title in 2006–07, beating out Jay Pandolfo of New Jersey and Samuel Pahlsson of Anaheim. Brind'Amour finished with 38 PCD points, tied for second in the league and better than his co-nominees. Pandolfo probably deserved his nomination, with 36 PCD points and a sixth overall finish. Pahlsson lagged behind with 30 PCD points, a respectable total but still outside of the top 10 in the league. Compared to 2005–06, the league did a reasonable job with its Selke nominees, but that begs the question: how could the nominations be almost spot-on one year, but completely miss the mark on a guy like Fisher in another? I guess we just have to accept that Fisher's nomination was absurd.

It's often thought that reputation is a huge factor in the voting for the more subjective NHL trophies, but the 2006–07 exclusion of Lehtinen brings that theory into question. Lehtinen is a four-time Selke winner, was nominated for the trophy in 2005–06 and had a stellar year according to PCD in 2006–07—yet he was completely ignored in that season's Selke nominations. The top 10 defensive forwards from 2006–07 were:

Player Contribution 2006–07: Top 10 Defensive Forwards			
Player	**Team**	**Position**	**PCD**
Pavel Datsyuk	DET	C	41
Brad Richards	TBL	C	38
Rod Brind'Amour	CAR	C	38
Jere Lehtinen	DAL	RW	36
Martin St. Louis	TBL	RW	36
Jay Pandolfo	NJD	LW	36
Craig Adams	CAR	RW	32
Alexander Steen	TOR	C	32
Chad LaRose	CAR	C	32
Simon Gagne	PHI	LW	31

Datsyuk led the way, and did so among all forwards in PCD for the second year in a row in 2007–08, this time winning the Selke after not being nominated in 2006–07. In that season, Datsyuk accumulated a PCD of 39 and a 132 PC total—far ahead of teammate Henrik Zetterberg and the Devils' John Madden, the other nominees that year. The voters were spot-on with Datsyuk, but not so great with the nominations as whole. Zetterberg and Madden tied for 20th in the league with 26 PCD points each. Ryder's system produces far more deserving candidates. Here are the top 10 defensive forwards of 2007–08:

Player Contribution 2007–08: Top 10 Defensive Forwards			
Player	Team	Position	PCD
Pavel Datsyuk	DET	C	39
Mike Grier	SJS	RW	36
Daymond Langkow	CGY	C	33
Martin St. Louis	TBL	RW	33
Jason Pominville	BUF	RW	32
Boyd Gordon	WAS	C	31
Joe Thornton	SJS	C	30
Ryan Johnson	STL	C	30
Viktor Kozlov	WAS	C	29
Alexander Steen	TOR	LW	28

Looking at the NHL's annual awards is a great demonstration of how hard it is to compare players and to rank and rate them. Doing so also provides a great platform for Ryder's currency, Player Contribution. PC puts a player's value into an easily interpreted number, something all fans can relate to. Ryder is the first to say that his methodology isn't perfect, but it is leaps and bounds ahead of using standard measures like goals and assists, statistics that are particularly useless when comparing, say, forwards to defensemen.

Player Contribution also shows how subjectivity can creep into decision-making—in this case deciding who is the best in the NHL in a variety of categories. The NHL heavily promotes its annual awards, but Ryder's work shows that the voters are prone to making mistakes. Perhaps in the future, the members of the PHWA will turn to a more objective method of measuring a player's ability than basic metrics and "gut feeling." The analysis shows they could use it.

Chapter Eight

Is Martin Brodeur Overrated?

Two Capitals defenders battle two Penguins forecheckers in the corner. The puck squirts free and defenseman Mike Green sends it up the boards, past the Pittsburgh point man and into the neutral zone. Alexander Ovechkin has a step on the Penguins' Rob Scuderi, and with Ovechkin's speed, the home crowd knows he won't be caught. Number 8 streaks in on the opposing goal at full speed. Scuderi makes a last-ditch attempt to stop the breakaway, diving, to no avail, at Ovechkin's feet. With a little hesitation, Ovechkin fakes a shot and makes a move to his forehand. A quick shot, a flash of leather, a magnificent save by goaltender Marc-Andre Fleury.

The box score's record: 1 shot, 1 save.

Later on in the same game, Pittsburgh forward Chris Kunitz dumps the puck into the Capitals' zone, and he and his linemates head to the bench for a line change. Tom Poti comes out from behind the Washington net with the puck and makes a sharp pass to winger Alexander Semin. Semin gets to the red line and snaps a 100-foot dump shot onto the Pittsburgh goal, where Fleury nonchalantly steers the puck to his defenseman.

The box score's record: 1 shot, 1 save.

Shots are a vital piece of the puzzle that is an NHL hockey game. The ability of a team to convert shots into goals is crucial to offense. But shots are also an important defensive measure, particularly to goaltenders. A goalie has one duty, and that's to keep pucks out of the net. The better a goaltender is, the more shots he is able to stop. However, as the introductory anecdote demonstrates, in a single game there are tremendous differences in the difficulty of shots the goalie will face.

The average NHL starting goaltender will see about 1600 shots over the course of a season. The difference between the best save percentage in the league and the 30th best is typically less than two percent. That means only about 30 saves separate the "best" goalie from the guy 29 positions lower. For a starting goaltender, that's likely less than one save per game over the course of a season. Putting shots and saves in this context stresses the importance of identifying the quality of a shot taken on a goalie. The lower the quality of shot faced, the easier the save and the better a goaltender's statistics will look. Thirty "easy" saves can transform a netminder from pretender to contender.

Theoretically, then, 1600 shots against one goalie are not necessarily equal to 1600 shots against another. Perhaps a goaltender plays a disproportionate amount of games against offensively futile teams. Or the converse, a goalie may play behind a spectacularly bad (or good) defense. Both of these situations will affect the quality of shots the goalie has to stop. But if all we see in the goaltender's data is a "shots on goal" column, how can we tell the difference between a goalie who faces tough shots and one who faces easier shots?

Play-by-Play Playa

In the 2002–03 season, the NHL began publishing play-by-play data. These data provided a chronological listing of the events of a hockey game, like this:

San Jose vs. Phoenix						
Event #	Per	Time	Event	Team	Type	Description
1	1	0:00	FACEOFF	N/A	-	PHX won - neutral zone. PHX 11 LANGKOW vs S.J 12 MARLEAU
2	1	0:17	SHOT	PHX	EV	12 JOHNSON, Slap, 64 ft
3	1	3:42	STOPPAGE	N/A	-	Puck in Netting
4	1	3:42	FACEOFF	N/A	-	S.J won - neutral zone. PHX 11 LANGKOW vs S.J 12 MARLEAU

Event #	Per	Time	Event	Team	Type	Description
San Jose vs. Phoenix cont.						
5	1	3:54	STOPPAGE	N/A	-	Puck in Crowd
6	1	3:54	FACEOFF	N/A	-	S.J won - offensive zone. PHX 11 LANGKOW vs S.J 12 MARLEAU
7	1	4:12	PENALTY	S.J	-	22 HANNAN, Hooking, 2 min
8	1	4:12	FACEOFF	N/A	-	PHX won - offensive zone. PHX 11 LANGKOW vs S.J 25 DAMPHOUSSE

Particularly useful was how the play-by-play record treated shots on goal. Instead of simply stating that a shot occurred, like a box score, the data listed the type of shot as well as the distance of it from the goal. This provided the eager analyst with a way to distinguish a dump-in on net from a breakaway. With just that minimal amount of information, the ever-industrious Alan Ryder set out to see if he could determine the differences in shot quality faced by NHL goaltenders.

After aggregating all the play-by-play data from the 2002–03 season, the questions confronting Ryder were what constituted an easy shot and what counted as a hard shot. He decided to divide the shot data by shot type—wrist, slap, snap, etc.—as well as by how far away from the goal the shot was taken. Then, by examining the actual results in the NHL's play-by-play reports, the probability of each shot resulting in a goal was modeled and calculated. For example, a slap shot taken from 10 feet away might score 20 percent of the time, while a backhand from 30 feet away might only score at a rate of two percent.

With this data in hand, Ryder then compared it to a team's real-life shot outcomes from the 2002–03 season. Each shot against had a specific probability of turning into a goal. The sum of all these probabilities, multiplied by the total shots faced by the team resulted in the number of goals that *should* have been scored on the team, according to the model. This comparison provided a reference point. If the data revealed that a team *should* have given up more (or fewer) goals than the league average, it was assumed that this team gave up more (or fewer) difficult shots. The ratio of expected goals against to league-average goals against provided a measure of the relative difficulty of the shots faced by a team. Ryder called this metric Shot Quality Against (SQA). With an SQA of 1.00, a team faced a shot difficulty equivalent to the league average. An SQA higher than 1.00—for example, 1.05—meant that a team gave up higher quality shots, five percent higher than the league average. You could interpret this as a weaker-than-average team defense. An SQA below 1.00, say 0.900, implied a better defense; this team's shots against were 10 percent easier than the league average.

What can we learn about goaltending from a method that tells us about an opponent's shot quality? Logic dictates that if a team allows higher-quality shots, the goalie of that team is going to appear worse than he actually is. Imagine two netminders, both of whom face 1600 shots and allow 150 goals, for identical 0.906 save percentages. When the shot data is analyzed, it turns out that one of the goalies faced an SQA of 1.05, the other 0.98. Since they both made the same number of saves and allowed the same number of goals, the better goalie has to be the one who faced the more difficult shots. The question is how much better said goalie is than the other who faced the easier shots.

Fortunately, Ryder's methodology provides us with an answer: Shot Quality Neutral Save Percentage (SQNSV). Essentially, SQNSV tells us the expected save percentage of a team, normalized for the league average Shot Quality Against. That might sound complicated, but what the formula does is "balance" save percentages based on how much easier or harder an opponent's shot quality is. An example from Ryder's work on shot quality demonstrates how this works: in 2002–03, Florida (mainly backstopped by Roberto Luongo) had a team save percentage of 0.913, good enough for eighth place in the NHL. But the Panthers gave up the second highest quality of shots in the league.

They had an SQA of 1.078, meaning the average shot against the Panthers was 7.8 percent more difficult than the league average. When SQA is accounted for via Ryder's methods, Florida jumps up into a tie for first place in SQNSV, at 0.919. In other words, when an opponent's shot quality was taken into account, Florida had the highest save percentage in the NHL, adjusted up to account for the higher quality of shots given up by the team. The team's goaltending statistics, measured by the league, were understated because of a weak defense.

Ryder provided a framework from which to analyze shot quality, but the data from the period restricted the examination to a team level. As the data improved, Ken Kryzwicki decided it was a good idea to revisit shot quality.

Making it Personal

Kryzwicki's first order of business was to see if he could improve on Ryder's methodology. To do this, Kryzwicki decided to remodel the goal probabilities based on a logistic function. Nine variables, like shot distance, shot type, period, situation and whether the shot was a rebound, were considered for the logistic regression model, with only four ending up as statistically significant, thus surviving for use in the model. What's a logistic regression model? Without risking a reader's eyes glazing over or their head exploding, suffice it to say that it's a fancy "line of best fit" through the data, based on a logistic function. Kryzwicki's new "line of best fit" was slightly better than what was used in the prior work of Ryder. In the world of statistical analysis, "slightly better" is how model-makers earn a living.

More interesting to the hockey fan is Kryzwicki's application of the shot quality analysis on an individual level. Whereas Ryder's work gave us metrics describing the Florida Panthers as a team, thanks to newly published data regarding individual players, Kryzwicki's effort allowed us to see exactly how well guys like Luongo performed. According to Kryzwicki, "What is important is how these goaltenders performed given their circumstances." The circumstances of which Kryzwicki spoke were the quality of the opposition's shots. Here's an example from his work, using NHL data from 2003–04: Luongo, still with the Panthers at that point, finished the season with a 0.931 save percentage. According to Kryzwicki's model, Luongo faced easier shots from the opposing teams in relation to the league average in 2003–04 (remember, he faced higher-quality shots in 2002–03). Therefore, Kryzwicki's model predicted that a league-average goaltender, in Luongo's situation, would stop shots at the rate of 0.912. Although his statistics were slightly inflated thanks to a lower SQA, he still outperformed expectations by about two percent (0.931 actual versus 0.912 predicted).

Now armed with methods that attempt to measure the relationship between shot quality and goaltender performance, we can answer our interesting—if inflammatory—question.

Is Martin Brodeur Overrated?

Brodeur has accumulated quite a number of accolades in his 15-year NHL career. After winning the Calder Trophy as the NHL's top rookie in 1993–94, Brodeur led the New Jersey Devils to the first of three Stanley Cups the following season. And the trophies piled up: four William M. Jennings awards for fewest goals against, four Vezina Trophies as the league's best goalie, 10 all-star game appearances, an Olympic gold medal in 2002 and a World Hockey Championship in 2004. Brodeur also has more wins than any goaltender in hockey history. And if that hasn't cemented his place in the pantheon of hockey, then the fact that he'll likely break Terry Sawchuk's record of 103 career shutouts in the near future—something Don Cherry once said was unbreakable—will. People are beginning to whisper about the possibility that Brodeur is the best goaltender ever.

But if there is one thing we've learned from the analysis of shot quality, it is that it's difficult to distinguish between a team's performance and the individual goaltender's. A poor defensive team can make a good goalie look bad, and a great defensive team can make a bad goalie look good. I'm not saying that Brodeur is a bad goaltender, but a quick review of his career reveals that he wins a lot of games (a very team-dependent statistic), gets a lot of shutouts (also team dependent) and the media and fans believe he's an amazing goaltender. But before we jump on the bandwagon and start calling him the best goalie in the history of the NHL, we need to see just how good he is at doing what goalies are supposed to do—and that's stopping opposing shots. Thanks to the work on shot quality, we can do that.

Although Ryder's work on the 2002–03 season was limited to team-wide data, it's still possible to use it to gain insight into the performance of individual goalies. This is especially so when dealing with a player like Brodeur, who plays such a high proportion of his team's games. Here's the data from that season:

SQA 2002–03		
Team	Shots Against	SQA
NJD	1765	0.915
PHI	1813	0.935
MIN	2047	0.947
CGY	1959	0.953
TOR	2129	0.956
TBL	2070	0.965
BUF	2087	0.969
OTT	1893	0.970
ANA	2126	0.972
DAL	1812	0.972
WAS	2174	0.973
DET	2131	0.976
PHX	2149	0.980
MTL	2417	0.982
CHI	2158	0.996
PIT	2222	0.996
NAS	2033	1.000
VAN	1985	1.004
EDM	2033	1.018
COL	2113	1.018
SJS	2178	1.022
CAR	2062	1.024
BOS	2087	1.027
NYI	2121	1.037
CLB	2400	1.041
ATL	2327	1.045
LAK	1921	1.048
NYR	2111	1.057

SQA 2002–03 cont.		
Team	Shots Against	SQA
FLA	2398	1.078
STL	1898	1.087

Recall that SQA is Shot Quality Against, and an SQA below 1.00 represents a team that allows lower-quality shots against; an SQA of greater than one represents higher-quality shots given up. According to Ryder's results, the New Jersey Devils had the best defense in the league, giving up the lowest quality of shots by quite a margin. As a team, the Devils had an SQA of 0.915. Thanks to their lower quality of shots against, Ryder's calculations establish an SQNSV value of 0.906. That drops New Jersey down to 14th in the league, right in the middle. The Devils' team save percentage, as calculated by the NHL, was overstated because of the lower-quality shots faced.

What does this mean for Brodeur? In 2002–03 Brodeur played in 73 of the team's 82 games. As such, his statistics fluctuate according to shot quality in a fashion similar to the team as a whole. Since Brodeur's actual save percentage was 0.914, slightly worse than the team's overall save percentage, his SQNSV is also approximately the same as the team's, about 0.906.

Brodeur's statistics are inflated by New Jersey's stellar defense.

Here are the top 25 goaltenders from the 2002–03 season, with a minimum of 30 games played, organized by save percentage:

Top 25 Goaltenders 2002–03		
Player	Team	SV%
Marty Turco	DAL	0.932
Dwayne Roloson	MIN	0.927
Roman Cechmanek	PHI	0.925
Manny Fernandez	MIN	0.924
Ed Belfour	TOR	0.922
Patrick Roy	COL	0.920
Jean-Sebastien Giguere	ANA	0.920
Olaf Kolzig	WAS	0.919
Roberto Luongo	FLA	0.918
Garth Snow	NYI	0.918
Tomas Vokoun	NAS	0.918
Mike Dunham	2Tm	0.916
Jocelyn Thibault	CHI	0.915
Martin Brodeur	NJD	0.914
Kevin Weekes	CAR	0.912
Curtis Joseph	DET	0.912
Jeff Hackett	2Tm	0.911
Patrick Lalime	OTT	0.911
Nikolai Khabibulin	TBL	0.911
John Grahame	2Tm	0.909
Dan Cloutier	VAN	0.908

Top 25 Goaltenders 2002–03 cont.		
Player	Team	SV%
Jose Theodore	MTL	0.908
Martin Biron	BUF	0.908
Robert Esche	PHI	0.907
Evgeni Nabokov	SJS	0.906

Before the statistic is adjusted, Brodeur is firmly entrenched in the middle of the pack, placing 14th out of the 25 goaltenders. But after adjusting save percentage for shot quality, a different tale emerges:

Top 25 Goaltenders 2002–03: SQNSV			
Player	Team	SQA	SQNSV
Marty Turco	DAL	0.972	0.930
Roberto Luongo	FLA	1.078	0.924
Dwayne Roloson	MIN	0.947	0.923
Patrick Roy	COL	1.018	0.921
Garth Snow	NYI	1.037	0.921
Roman Cechmanek	PHI	0.935	0.920
Manny Fernandez	MIN	0.947	0.920
Mike Dunham	2Tm	1.040	0.919
Ed Belfour	TOR	0.956	0.918
Tomas Vokoun	NAS	1.000	0.918
Jean-Sebastien Giguere	ANA	0.972	0.918
Olaf Kolzig	WAS	0.973	0.917
Jocelyn Thibault	CHI	0.996	0.915
Kevin Weekes	CAR	1.024	0.914
John Grahame	2Tm	1.010	0.910

Top 25 Goaltenders 2002–03: SQNSV cont.			
Player	Team	SQA	SQNSV
Curtis Joseph	DET	0.976	0.910
Jeff Hackett	2Tm	0.985	0.910
Dan Cloutier	VAN	1.004	0.908
Patrick Lalime	OTT	0.970	0.908
Evgeni Nabokov	SJS	1.022	0.908
Nikolai Khabibulin	TBL	0.965	0.908
Jose Theodore	MTL	0.982	0.906
Martin Brodeur	NJD	0.915	0.906
Martin Biron	BUF	0.969	0.905
Robert Esche	PHI	0.935	0.901

Save percentage is probably the best measure of a goaltender's ability to do what we expect a goalie to do, which is stop pucks. Goals against average (GAA) isn't great because it's possible for a goalie to play on a horrible team, stand on his head every game and still "average" more goals against than the rest of the league. Wins and losses are purely a product of the team. There are certainly times when a netminder is the root cause of a win, but there are also plenty of other instances when a goalie is merely a cog in the wheel. And since a goalie is responsible for only one part of the hockey game—defense—it's impossible for him to single-handedly win a game. Shutouts are somewhat indicative of a goalie's skill, but they are also a function of both a goalie's ability to stop pucks and the team's ability to prevent dangerous shots. All things being equal, a goalie on a good defensive team will get more shutouts than a goalie on a poor defensive team.

That leaves us with save percentage. By itself it isn't perfect, but when we adjust for the quality of shots taken, it appears to do a decent job of measuring a goaltender's performance. According to the adjusted statistic, SQNSV, Brodeur wasn't the best goalie in 2002–03. Nor was he second best. Or third. Brodeur plummeted all the way to 23rd place on the list. Is his standing a good representation of his value as a goalie or just indicative of a bad season?

According to Kryzwicki's work on shot quality, Brodeur's mediocre performance in 2002–03 was not an outlier. Kryzwicki's analysis revealed that Brodeur once again faced easier-than-average shot quality in 2003–04. And while Brodeur slightly outperformed expectations (0.917 actual versus 0.915 predicted, accounting for SQA), many of his contemporaries did far better when compared to league-average goaltending. Of the goaltenders who faced 1000 shots or more, 16 exceeded their predicted save percentage by more than Brodeur's 0.22 percent.

The pattern was the same after the NHL lockout of 2004. In the first season back on the ice,

Brodeur ranked behind 10 other netminders with 1000 or more shots against in terms of adjusted save percentage. Later, in his 2007–08 campaign, Brodeur, in second place, put up an SQNSV of 0.918, but it wasn't enough to displace first-place Tomas Vokoun, and Brodeur's great performance was not maintained. His SQNSV in 2008–09, tracked by the statistics site at the Hockey Numbers weblog, was a ho-hum 0.916, good enough for 13th spot in the league.

In the five seasons that shot quality was analyzed here, Brodeur failed to lead the league—ever—in adjusted save percentage (SQNSV), currently one of the best measures of a goaltender's ability. In fact, Brodeur only cracked the top 10 in the statistic once, in 2007–08. Does that sound like the résumé of someone considered as the possible *best goalie of all time*?

I think it's necessary to take a step back and re-examine this argument. I have no doubt that Brodeur is an extremely good, if not great, NHL goaltender. However, whereas he does exception- ally well in team-based counting statistics, like wins and shutouts, he is pretty average when it comes to individual performance measures. Where Brodeur really shines is in durability; between 1993–94 and 2008–09, he played in 995 games. That's 226 more games than the goalie with the next highest total over the same time span. That kind of stable, predictable performance is hugely valuable. Brodeur's resilience makes me think of Mike Gartner, one the most consistent goal scorers ever seen in the NHL. Gartner scored 30 goals or more for 15 years in a row (and had he not gotten injured, that streak would have likely extended to 17). That's absolutely amazing, but alas, no one is talking about Gartner as the best goal scorer of all time.

Despite the evidence against Brodeur, he will continue to gain traction in the "best ever" argument, most notably when he surpasses Sawchuk's record for career shutouts. But I'm not alone in the belief that Brodeur might be overrated. The Contrarian Goaltender, the blogger behind the relevantly titled website Brodeur is a Fraud, spends his days trying to educate the layman that the team has a heavy influence on the statistics of an individual goaltender, and that Brodeur may be the best example of this. The Contrarian Goaltender provides some compelling evidence. For starters, he argues that throughout Brodeur's career, he has benefited from a better-than-average team, resulting in better-than-average team-influenced statistics, like wins and shutouts. The New Jersey Devils are notorious for their defensive play, and are responsible for introducing the "neutral-zone trap" into the household lexicon. The system, introduced to the Devils by coach Jacques Lemaire in the late 1990s, worked wonders for the team, and Brodeur specifically. The stifling defensive strategy flummoxed the offense of opposing teams, easing the workload on the New Jersey netminders, who faced around 20 percent fewer shots against than the league average. Fewer shots means more wins and more shutouts, regardless of who's standing between the pipes.

There are ways to demonstrate just how well the Devils' defensive system works. When Lemaire left New Jersey to coach the Minnesota Wild, he took his approach with him. Despite being an expansion team, the Wild put up some good defensive numbers. In their first five seasons, the team finished last place in their division four times. However, they never allowed more goals against than the league average, finishing three times in the top five in that measure. When the Contrarian Goaltender compared the statistics of the Wild as a team against Brodeur's individual stats from 2000 to 2006, he found that the numbers were similar. Two great defensive teams produced equally great results from their goaltenders.

The criticism of Brodeur can also be approached from a different angle. If a team's defensive ability is excellent, then in theory, any goaltender should perform better behind said team. This is exactly what the Contrarian Goaltender discovered about Brodeur's backups, who put up similar save percentages, goals against averages and shutouts when compared to the Man himself. One of those backups was Corey Schwab. Before landing himself a gig with the New Jersey Devils, playing behind Brodeur, Schwab had an underwhelming career, consisting of a 3.13 GAA, 0.896 save percentage and four shutouts over 123 games. After getting to play behind the New Jersey Devils and the stifling trap, the Contrarian Goaltender found Schwab's stats improved dramatically; after 24 games with the Devils he had a 1.54 GAA, 0.929 save percentage and two shutouts. Even though this sample is small, Schwab's numbers are of the MVP variety, providing evidence that playing behind a great defense pumps up a goaltender's stats.

The Contrarian Goaltender continues to pile up the arguments. Brodeur faces fewer power-play shots against than other goaltenders because of the Devils' uncanny discipline that results in fewer penalties. His playoff statistics in what many fans consider "clutch" situations aren't amazing. He faces lower-quality chances according to SQA. The Vezina awards Brodeur has won had more deserving candidates. And the most conclusive piece of evidence against the "Brodeur: best ever" argument is probably that despite being a great goalie, he isn't even close to the best of his generation.

It took Dominik Hasek until the age of 28 before he managed to prove to his superiors that he deserved a starting job, getting his chance after Buffalo teammate Grant Fuhr was injured. From that moment on, Hasek was lights out. He led the league in save percentage six seasons in a row, and during that amazing streak, he won the Hart and Lester B. Pearson trophies twice (a first for a goaltender), won six Vezina trophies, earned three Jennings Awards and was a five-time First Team All-star. He led the 1999 Czech National Team to a gold medal at the Nagano Olympics on the strength of a 0.961 save percentage and an amazing 0.97 GAA in six games. He led the seventh-seeded Buffalo Sabres of 1998–99 to the Stanley Cup final, where they lost to the Dallas Stars in six games thanks to one of the most controversial goals of all time.

Yet, despite these accolades, Hasek's name isn't kicked around in the same way Brodeur's is. Hasek, instead, managed to earn himself a reputation as a whiner among many NHL fans. The basis for this was the open dispute between Hasek and Sabres coach Ted Nolan during the late '90s that eventually led to Nolan, a fan favorite, leaving the team. Many hockey fans believe that Hasek's heart was never really in the NHL and that he saved his best hockey for international play. He was also labeled, perhaps deservedly, as soft, removing himself from games and moving on and off the injured reserve late in his career. Hasek had a relatively short peak, the result of not becoming a starting NHL goaltender until 1993, 10 years after being drafted by the Chicago Blackhawks. Of course, Hasek had no control over many of these matters, and none should overshadow the fact that his goaltending skills were uncanny. The statistics don't lie.

When Brodeur's age 29–34 seasons are compared with those of Hasek at the same ages—a likeness that analyzes both players in their natural prime—the numbers side-by-side are not even close. According to the Contrarian Goaltender, Hasek faced nearly 1500 more shots than Brodeur while allowing 41 fewer goals. Hasek's Buffalo Sabres averaged 22 minutes in penalties per game, while the Devils averaged only 11, which resulted in far more power-play opportunities against the former. And what about each goalie's respective backups? Hasek's had a 3.31 GAA and 0.897 save percentage, far worse than Hasek himself, while Brodeur's managed to achieve a respectable 2.21 GAA and 0.910 save percentage. Finally, the Dominator retired with a 0.925 *career* save percentage, a number Brodeur has only achieved in one season so far in his career.

So, is Brodeur overrated? I guess that depends on how you rate him. Based on statistics, I don't think he can be considered the best goalie of all time, yet so many fans refuse to believe it. Why? I think it's a combination of factors. Brodeur's a great goalie who plays in a large American market, but he is also renowned in Canada for his National Team heroics. He's well-liked by fans, the media and his NHL peers, which is in part helped by the fact that he's played his entire NHL career for a single team. And, although the records Brodeur has broken are heavily team-influenced, they shouldn't be brushed off entirely—we all know fans love records.

Yes, Brodeur is many things, but I maintain that the "best" definitely isn't one of them.

Conclusion

The intention of this book wasn't to change your mind about specific players or teams. Rather, I wanted to introduce you to the world of statistical analysis within hockey. With this introduction, I hope I gave you a small insight into how this breed of hockey analyst thinks, as well as demonstrated how the simplest of statistical techniques can transform a point a view.

Hockeynomics isn't only for hard-core numbers guys or professional statisticians; it's for hockey fans of all flavors. The purpose of this field is to better understand the game of hockey, and in order to increase our understanding of it we have to measure and examine it in new and exciting ways.

But if you want to enjoy hockey under this new paradigm, are you required to sit in front of a computer, spreadsheet software open? Of course not. All you need is an open mind and the realization that sometimes there are better indicators of "good" or "bad" than just gut feelings. Looking at the meager-but-continually-increasing amount of NHL data available and the statistical manipulation thereof is a great method for finding those indicators.

If I've piqued your interest or induced a hunger for this type of work, don't worry; in "Further Reading" I've included a small selection of recommended websites and books for you to check into. Within their pages, paper or virtual, you'll find a ton of fantastic analysis—more (and better) work than what can realistically fit into a book of this scope.

History suggests that the advanced analysis of hockey is inevitable, so get ready for it. Visit the sites and read the books. Examine the numbers objectively. Think, opine, discuss and argue. Challenge everything. For if we, as fans, can't participate in these activities, what is hockey but an absurd game consisting of skates, sticks and a vulcanized piece of rubber?

Key to Abbreviations

+/−:	*Plus/Minus*
$/GC:	*Cost per Goals Created*
A:	*Assists*
Act. Win%:	*Actual win percentage*
ADJ TOI:	*Adjusted Time on Ice*
ATOI:	*Average time on ice*
ADJ GC/60:	*Adjusted Goals Created per 60 minutes*
ES TOI:	*Even-strength time on ice*
Ex. Win%:	*Expected win percentage*
G:	*Goals*
GA:	*Goals against*
GAA:	*Goals against average*
GC:	*Goals Created*
GF:	*Goals for*
GP:	*Games played*
G/60:	*Goals per 60 minutes*
G/Min:	*Goals per minute*
GC/60:	*Goals Created per 60 minutes*
GC/G:	*Goals Created per Game*
GP/NHL:	*Games played in NHL*
GP/Pick:	*Games Played per NHL Pick*
KGCA:	*Kinda Goals Created Against*
KGCA/60:	*Kinda Goals Created Against per 60 minutes*
MP/MW:	*Marginal Payroll/Marginal Wins*
Net G/60:	*Net Goals per 60 minutes*
Net GC/$1 MM:	*Net Goals created per $1 million*
P:	*Points*

PC: *Player Contribution points*

PCD: *Player Contribution points on defense*

PCO: *Player Contribution points on offense*

PCOEV: *Player Contribution points at even-strength*

PCOPPO: *Player Contribution points by creating power-play opportunities*

PCOPPP: *Player Contribution points during power-play production*

PCOSH: *Player Contribution points during short-handed situations*

PGA: *Player's Goals Against*

PIM: *Penalties in minutes*

PPG: *Power-play goals*

PP TOI: *Power-play time on ice*

P/60: *Points per 60 minutes*

SH TOI: *Short-handed time on ice*

SOG: *Shots on goal*

SPCT: *Shot percentage*

SQA: *Shot Quality Against*

SQNSV: *Shot Quality Neutral Save Percentage*

SV%: *Save percentage*

TGA: *Team Goals Against*

TOI: *Time on ice*

TPGA: *Total Player's Goals Against*

TOI(M): *Time on ice (minutes)*

Further Reading

Websites

Though the world of hockey analysis remains underground, scattered around the Internet are a number of sites that dedicate themselves to the objective examination of hockey:

Hockey Analytics
www.hockeyanalytics.com

The home of Alan Ryder. Contains many papers published by Ryder, as well as those by other authors.

Hockey Numbers
hockeynumbers.blogspot.com

Chris Boersma's site, featuring a frequently updated weblog as well as his statistics site where you can find some unique hockey metrics.

Hockey Reference
www.hockey-reference.com

THE place to go for hockey statistics. Wonderfully laid out and extremely rich in information.

Hockey Prospectus
www.puckprospectus.com

The most recent addition to the Prospectus family of sports analysis sites. Full of objectively based articles by a great team of writers, including Iain Fyffe.

Behind The Net
www.behindthenet.ca

Hockey Prospectus author Gabriel Desjardin's personal website. Desjardin has completed some great work trying to establish the "quality of competition" for NHL hockey players.

Battle of Alberta
battleofalberta.blogspot.com

A witty weblog that focuses on the two Alberta teams: the Edmonton Oilers and Calgary Flames.

Brodeur is a Fraud
brodeurisafraud.blogspot.com

Site run by the anonymously monikered "Contrarian Goaltender"—and with such an inflammatory title, it's easy to understand why the author of it chooses to remain nameless. Great objective hockey analysis, slanted towards the guys between the pipes.

MC79 Hockey
www.mc79hockey.com

Objective and humorous weblog centered around the Edmonton Oilers. Great commenting section.

The Hockey Database
www.hockeydb.com

If there's a public record of a person playing hockey—anywhere—this is where to find his statistics.

NHL Numbers
www.nhlnumbers.com

The best resource on the Internet for player salaries and team payrolls.

Books

***The Numbers Game* by Alan Schwarz**
Schwarz wrote the book on our fascination with statistics, chronicling more than 100 years of baseball.

***Moneyball* by Michael Lewis**
The book that brought the statistical strategies of sports into the mainstream. A great read.

***Win Shares, The New Historical Baseball Abstract* by Bill James**
…or anything else you can get your hands on by this pioneer in the field.

Darcy Norman

Born and raised in Espanola, Ontario, and with no shortage of ice in the winter, Darcy has lived and breathed hockey since he was five years old. Playing from Tykes to the Junior level, this University of Alberta Economics major has retained his passion for the game by turning it into a study that reflects his educational pursuits involving numbers and data analysis. He strongly believes that reading numbers is the only truly objective method of analysis, be it on the stock market or on the sports page. Darcy is also the author of *Hockey Stats and Facts 2008–09*.